USBORNE FIRST BOOK OF NATURE

ROSAMUND KIDMAN COX
BARBARA CORK
and RUTH THOMSON

Designed by DAVID BENNETT

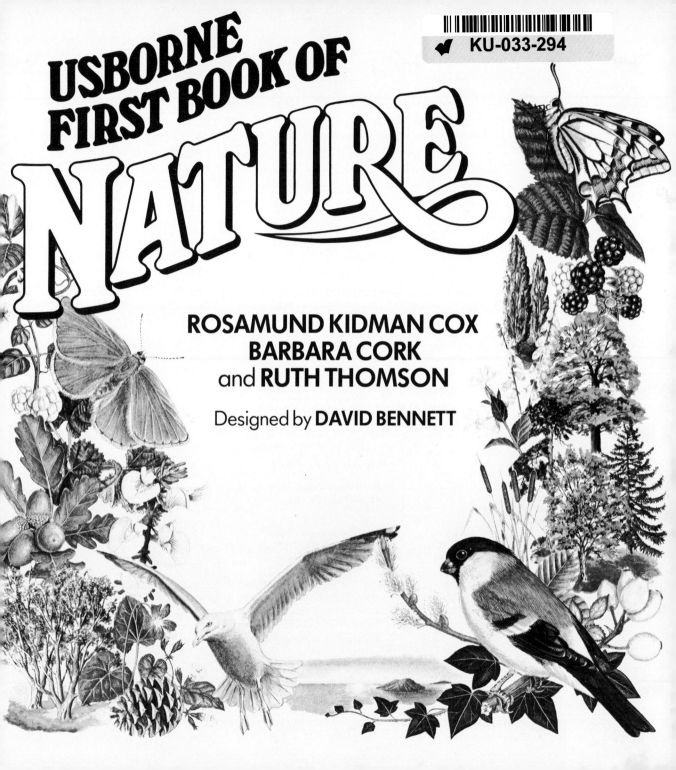

USBORNE FIRST BOOK OF NATURE

Illustrated by

Bob Bampton *(The Garden Studio)* · Joyce Bee · Wendy Bramall *(Artist Partners)* · Paul Brooks *(John Martin Artists)* · Mark Burgess · Frankie Coventry *(Artist Partners)* · Michelle Emblem *(Middletons)* · Denise Finney · Sarah Fox-Davies · Sheila Galbraith · Victoria Goaman · David Hurrell *(Middletons)* · Roy Hutchison *(Middletons)* · Elaine Keenan · Richard Lewington *(The Garden Studio)* · Mick Loates *(The Garden Studio)* · Andy Martin · Dee McLean *(Linden Artists)* · David More *(Linden Artists)* · Dee Morgan · Robert Morton *(Linden Artists)* · Liz Pepperell *(The Garden Studio)* · Cynthia Pow *(Middletons)* · Chris Shields *(Wilcock Riley)* · John Sibbick *(John Martin Artists)* · Ralph Stobart · John Thompson-Steinkrauss *(John Martin Artists)* · Sally Voke *(Middletons)* · James Woods *(Middletons)* ·

Language Consultant

Betty Root

Consultant Editors

Peter Olney

Esmond Harris B.Sc., Dip. For., F.I.For.,
Director of the Royal Forestry Society
of England, Wales and Northern Ireland.

Mary Gibby Ph.D.

Anthony Wootton
and David Carter

First published in 1980
by Usborne Publishing Ltd, 20 Garrick Street,
London WC2

Printed in Belgium

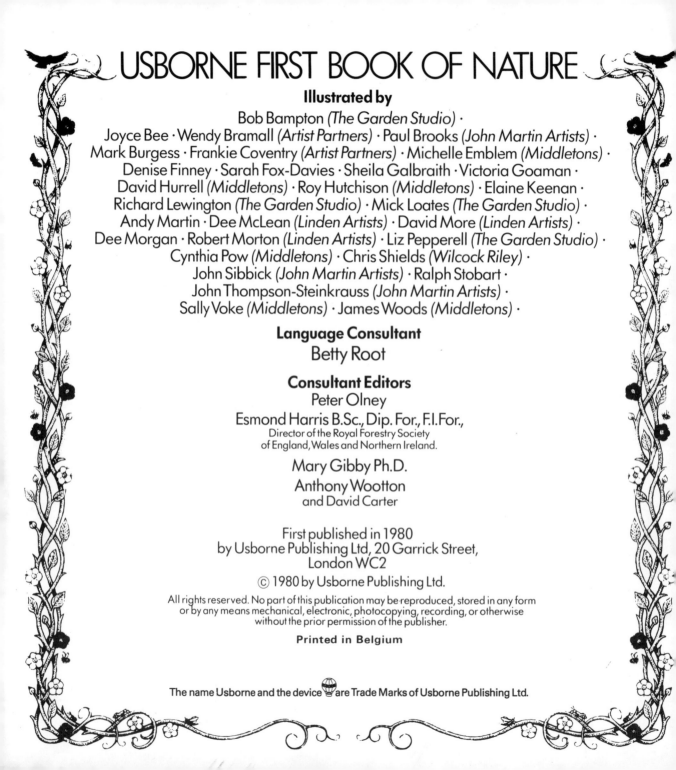

BIRDS

Games

1. Hunt the Grasshopper

Some birds eat Grasshoppers. Can you find 13 more Grasshoppers in the bird pages?

2. Watch the bird fly

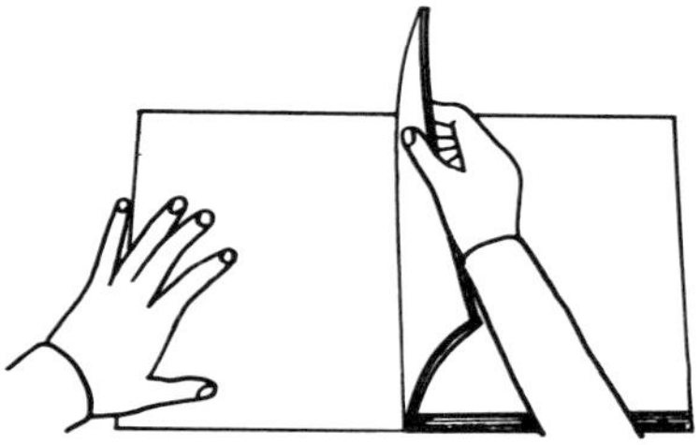

Hold the Bird pages like this.

Watch the top right hand corner and flick the pages over fast.

Looking at birds

A bird is like
an aeroplane.

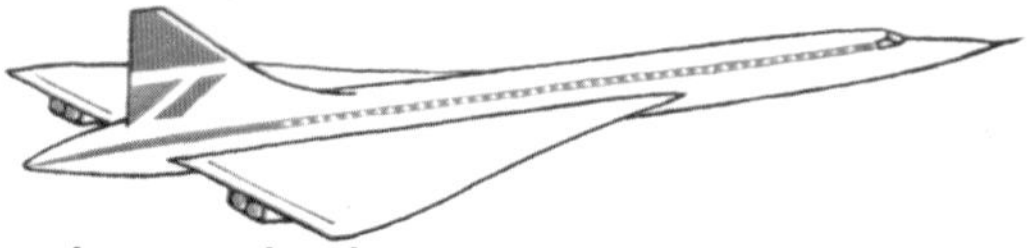

Its shape helps it to
move fast through the air.

A bird is like
a bat.

It uses its arms
as wings.

Swallow

A bird is like
a weightlifter.
It has strong arm
and chest muscles.

A bird is like
a balloon.
It has lots of air
inside its body.

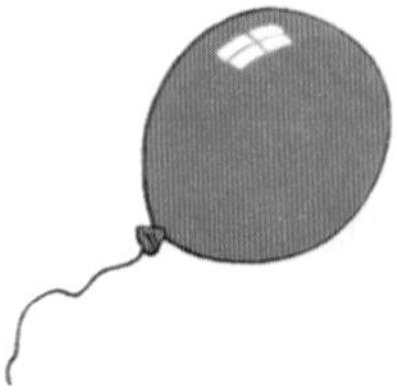

Birds are the only
animals in the world
that have feathers.

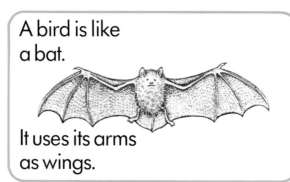

Birds have three kinds of feathers.

1. Down feathers.
They help keep the bird warm.

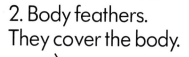

2. Body feathers.
They cover the body.

3. Flight feathers.
They help the bird to fly.

Greylag goose

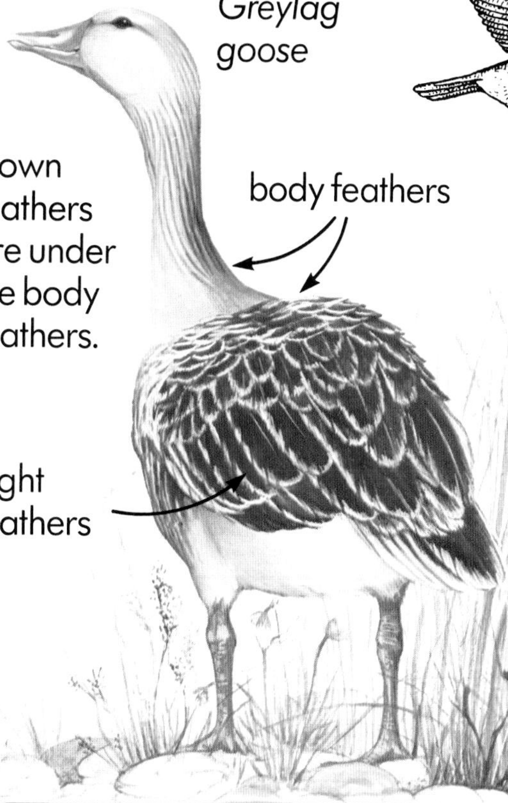

Birds grow a new set of feathers every year.

A goose cannot fly while its new flight feathers are growing.

baby goose

Baby birds have down feathers to help keep them warm.

Taking off and flying

Blue Tit

When birds want to take off, they leap into the air and flap their wings as fast as they can.

Mute Swan

Some birds are too heavy to leap into the air. Before they can take off they have to run along flapping their wings.

Bee-eater

Hummingbird

Wood Warbler

Mallard

Tawny Owl

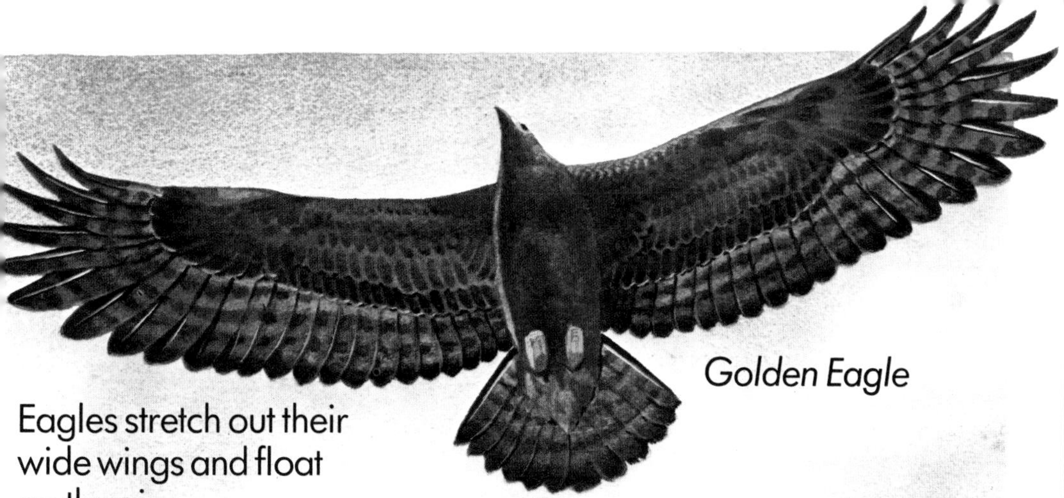

Golden Eagle

Eagles stretch out their wide wings and float on the air.

Large birds, like eagles, flap their wings slowly. Small birds flap their wings very fast.

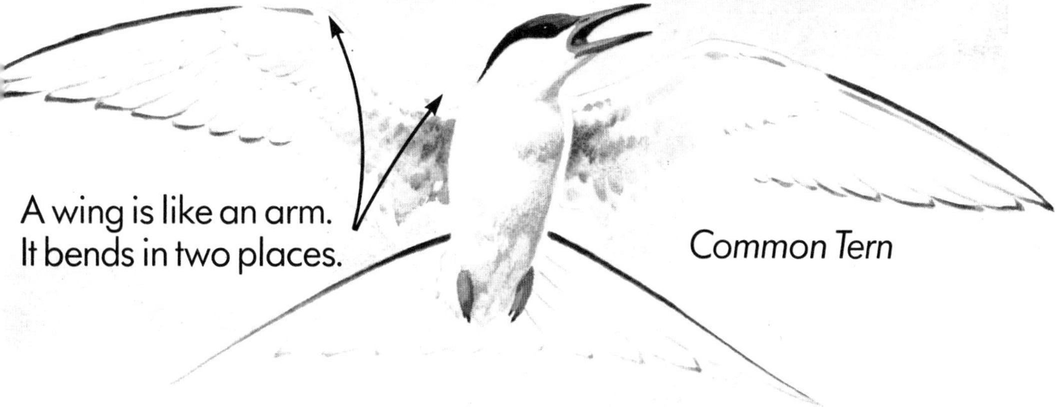

A wing is like an arm. It bends in two places.

Common Tern

Birds twist or bend their wings to turn in the air. Look at the way the other birds on this page bend their wings.

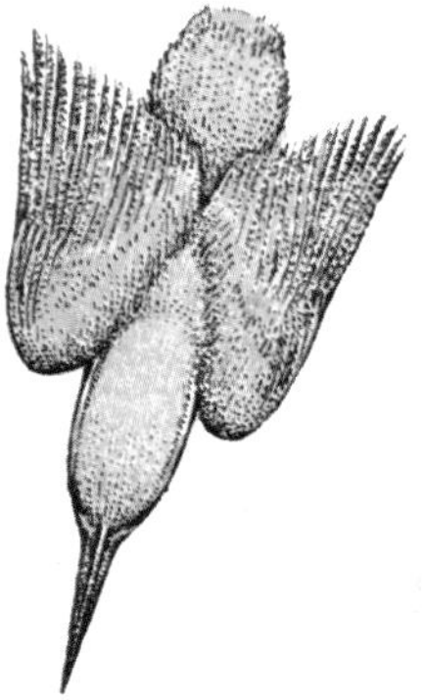

Kingfisher

Galah

Goldfinch

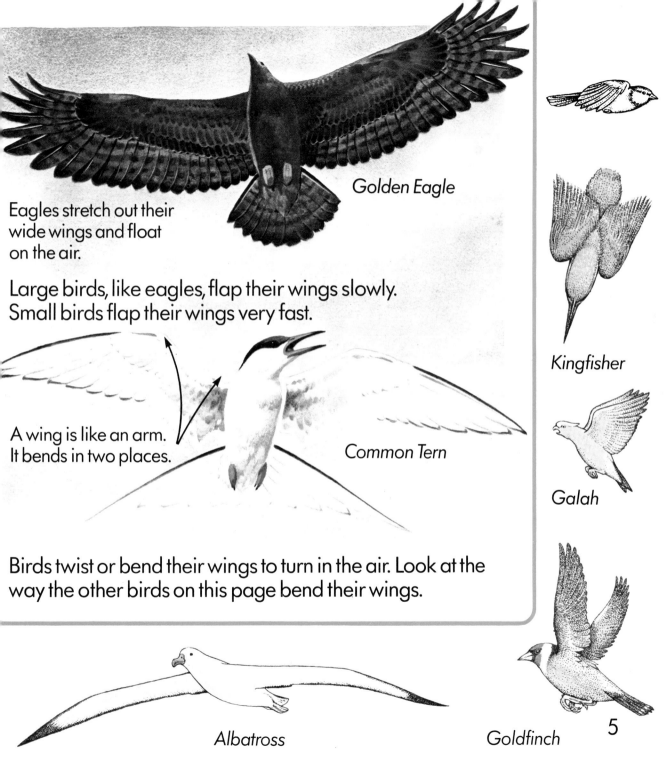

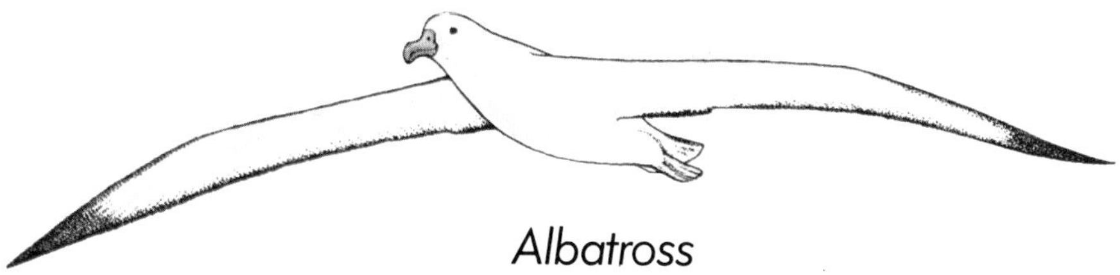

Albatross

Why do birds fly?

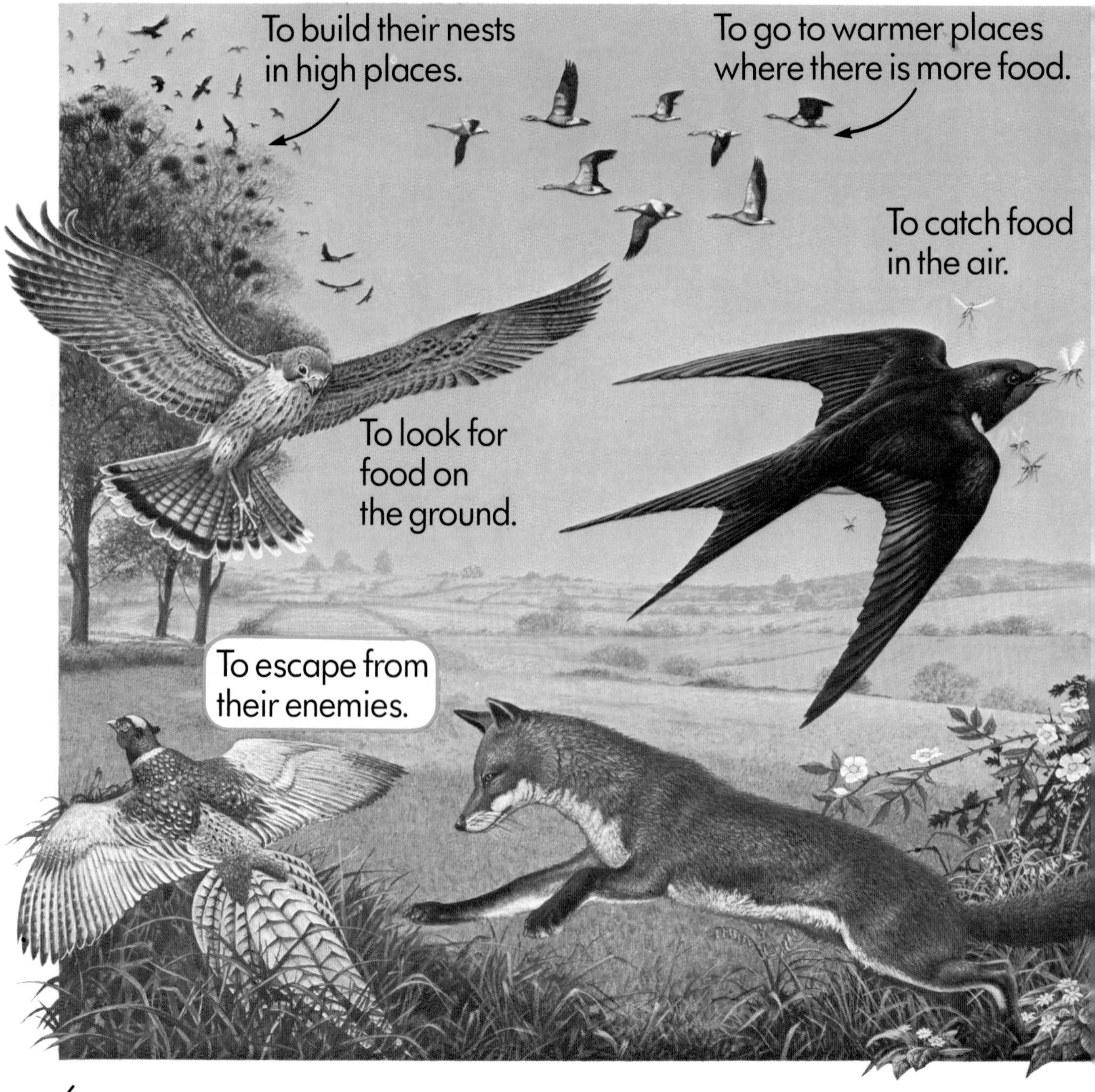

To build their nests in high places.
To go to warmer places where there is more food.
To catch food in the air.
To look for food on the ground.
To escape from their enemies.

Why do birds land?

Legs and feet

Puffin

A bird puts out its feet to land.
It also spreads out its tail and wings to slow down.

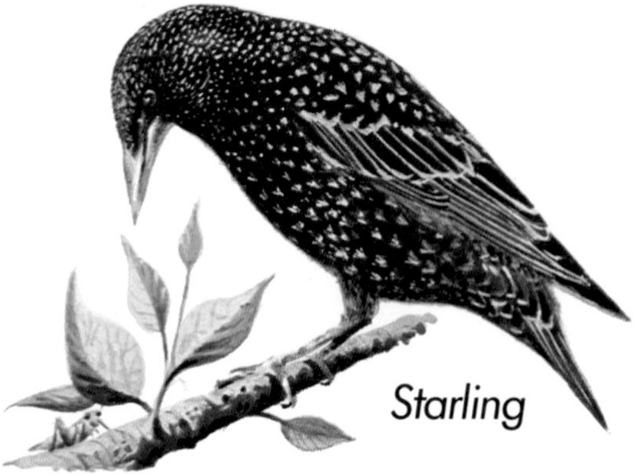

Starling

This bird rests on branches.
When it bends its legs,
its toes lock on to the branch.

Birds walk on their toes.
They can run or hop along the ground.

A bird's leg bends here.

Marabou Stork

Some birds rest on the ground.
Storks often sit like this when they rest.

Water birds have skin between their toes. The skin helps them to use their feet as paddles and to walk on mud without sinking in.

Snowy Owl
The feathers on
its feet help it
to walk on the snow
without sinking in.

The Snowy Owl has claws like daggers. It kills with its feet. Its feet are covered with feathers to keep them warm.

Beaks and feeding

Birds have no teeth so they cannot chew food. They swallow food whole and then grind it up in their stomachs.

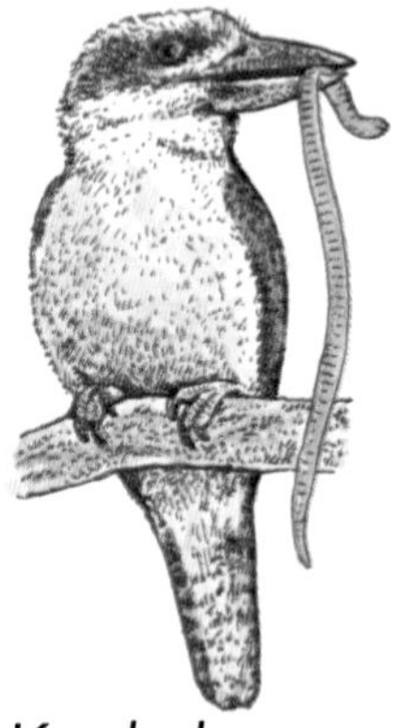

Kookaburra

Magpie

Crossbill

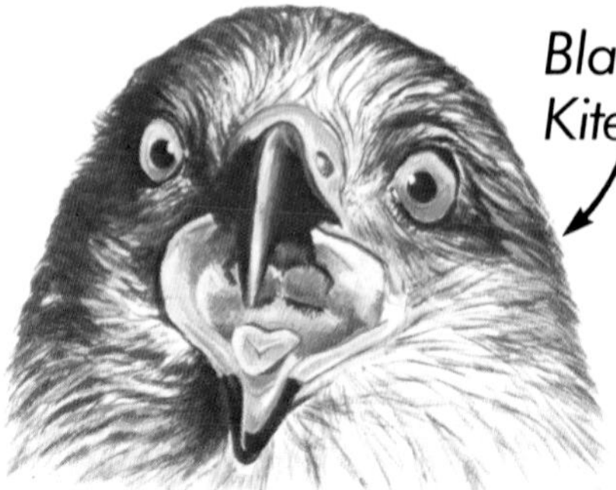

Black Kite

This bird uses its hooked beak to tear up its food.

Shoveler

This duck uses its beak as a strainer. It collects tiny plants and animals from the top of the water.

Pelicans

A Pelican uses its huge beak to scoop fish from the water. Its beak can hold more food than its stomach.

Hummingbird

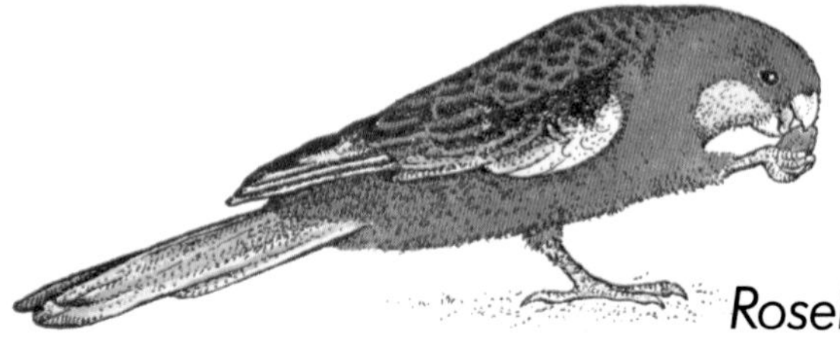

Rosella

Birds have different kinds of beaks because they eat different kinds of food. These seashore birds can feed close together because they eat different animals.

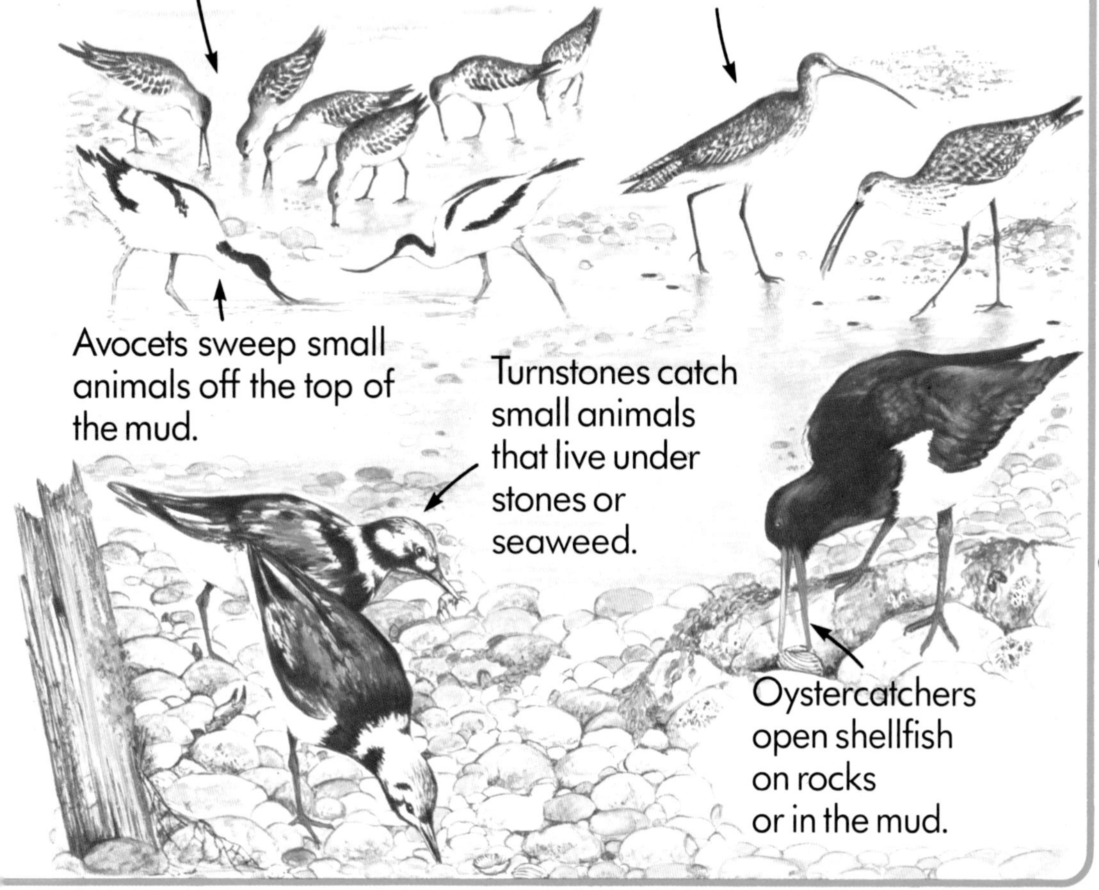

Godwits poke their beaks a short way into the mud to catch small animals.
Curlews have very long beaks. They eat animals that live deep in the mud.
Avocets sweep small animals off the top of the mud.
Turnstones catch small animals that live under stones or seaweed.
Oystercatchers open shellfish on rocks or in the mud.

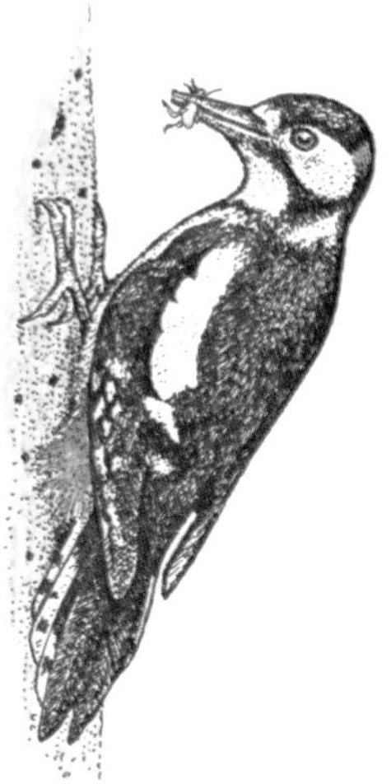

Woodpecker

Splendid Wren

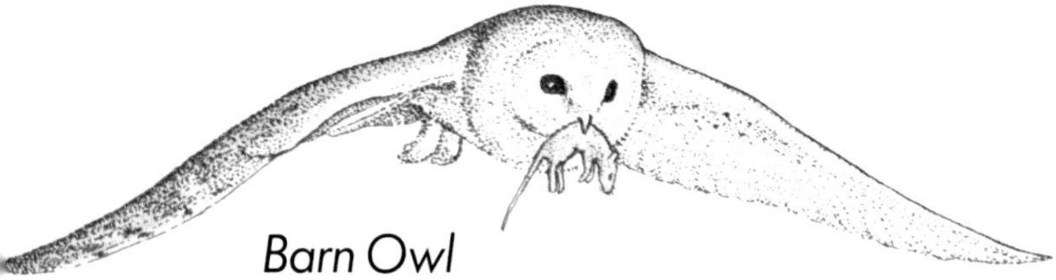

Barn Owl

Wigeon

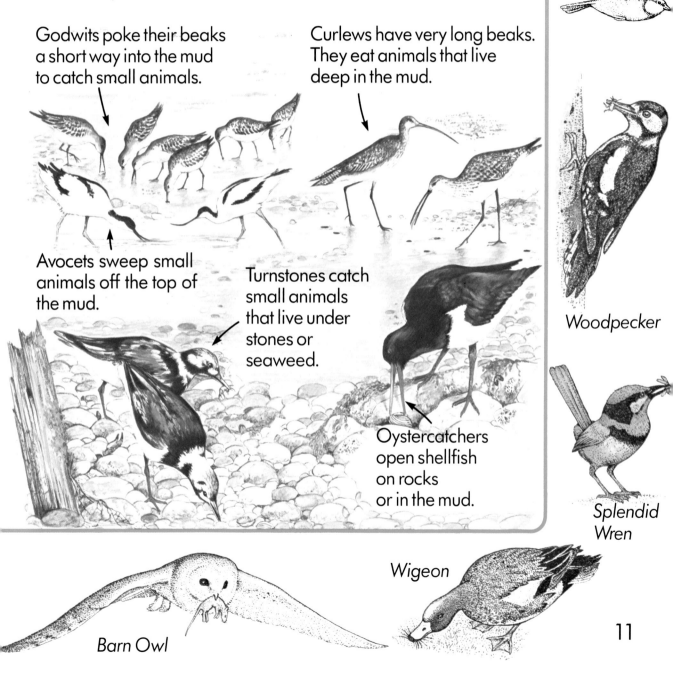

Colours

Many birds match the colour of the leaves and branches of the trees they rest in. This helps them to hide from their enemies.

There are seven birds in this picture.
Can you see them all?

When birds are sitting on eggs, they need to be hidden. This female Nightjar is sitting on her eggs. She is hard to see.

The Australian Frogmouth sleeps all day in a tree. It sits very still with its head up. It looks just like a broken branch.

Birds may use their colours to recognize each other.

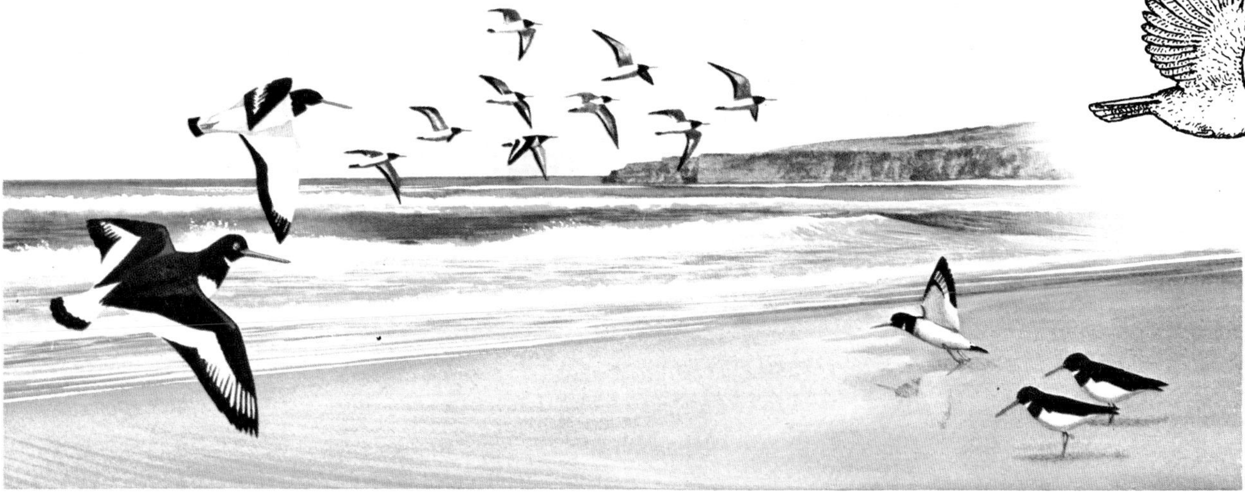

Oystercatchers live together in big groups. If some of the birds fly off to a new feeding place, the others soon follow. They recognize each other by their colours and the calls that they make.

Male and female Mallards are different colours. Male Mallards are most colourful in the breeding season. They show off their bright colours in a special dance. This attracts a female for mating.

Song and dance

Birds sing most of all in the breeding season.

Male Blackbirds sing to attract female Blackbirds.

female Blackbird

Male Blackbirds also sing to tell other male Blackbirds "This is where I live so keep away".

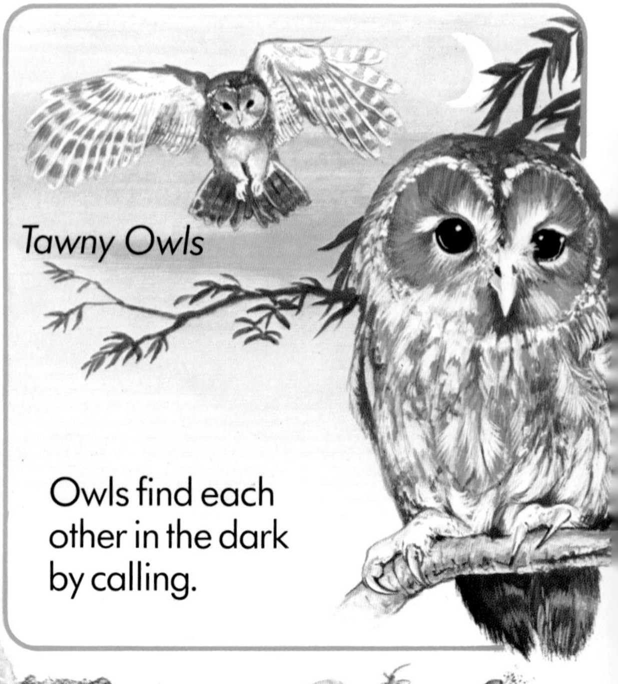

Tawny Owls

Owls find each other in the dark by calling.

The male Pigeon has to dance in front of the female before he can mate with her. He turns in circles and "coos" loudly all the time.

1. The male makes himself look big. He puffs out his neck feathers.

2. He spreads out his tail like a fan and bows to the female.

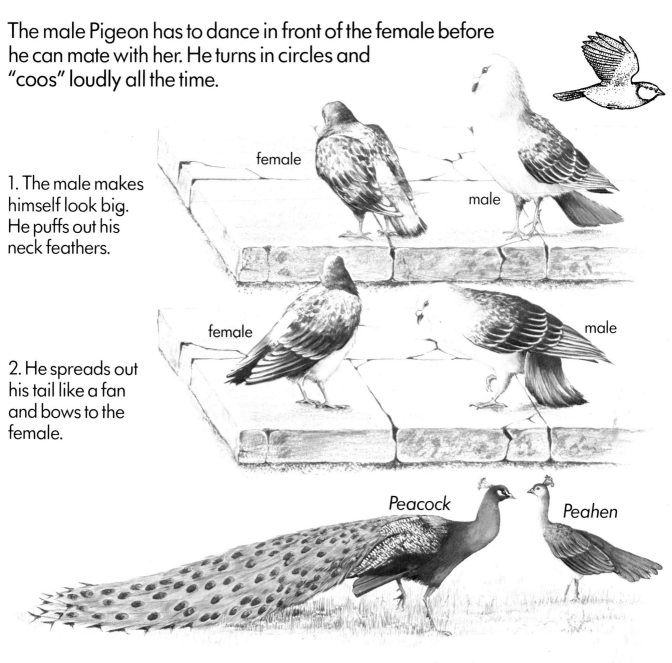

The peacock uses his long feathers in a dance to attract a female. The long feathers fall out when the breeding season is over.

Eggs and nests

Soon after a female bird has mated, she lays her eggs. If she kept all her eggs inside her until they were ready to hatch, she would probably be too heavy to fly.

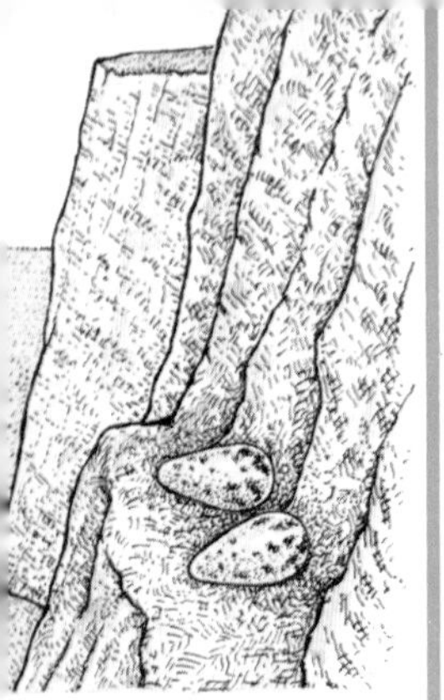

Guillemot eggs

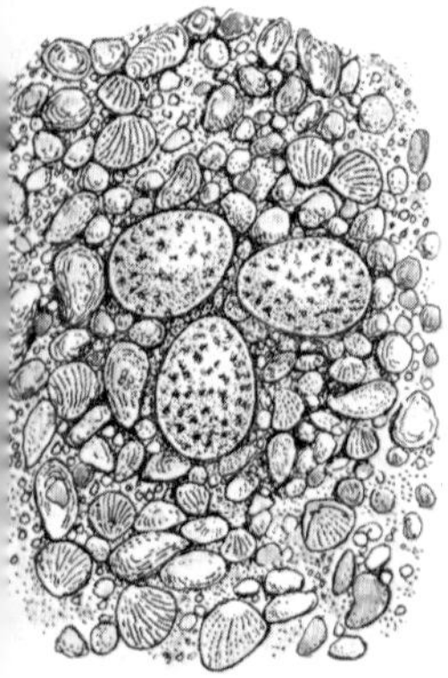

Oystercatcher eggs

The female Common Tern lays her eggs on the ground. A baby Tern grows inside each egg.

The eggs match the colour of the ground around them. It is hard for enemies to see them.

When baby Terns hatch, they are covered with down. The down helps keep them warm.

If an enemy is about, the baby Terns crouch down so they are difficult to see.

Rook eggs

Eider Duc eggs

Most birds build nests. The nest hides the eggs and baby birds from enemies. It helps to keep them warm. Birds also sit on their eggs to keep them warm. If the eggs get cold, the baby birds inside them will die.

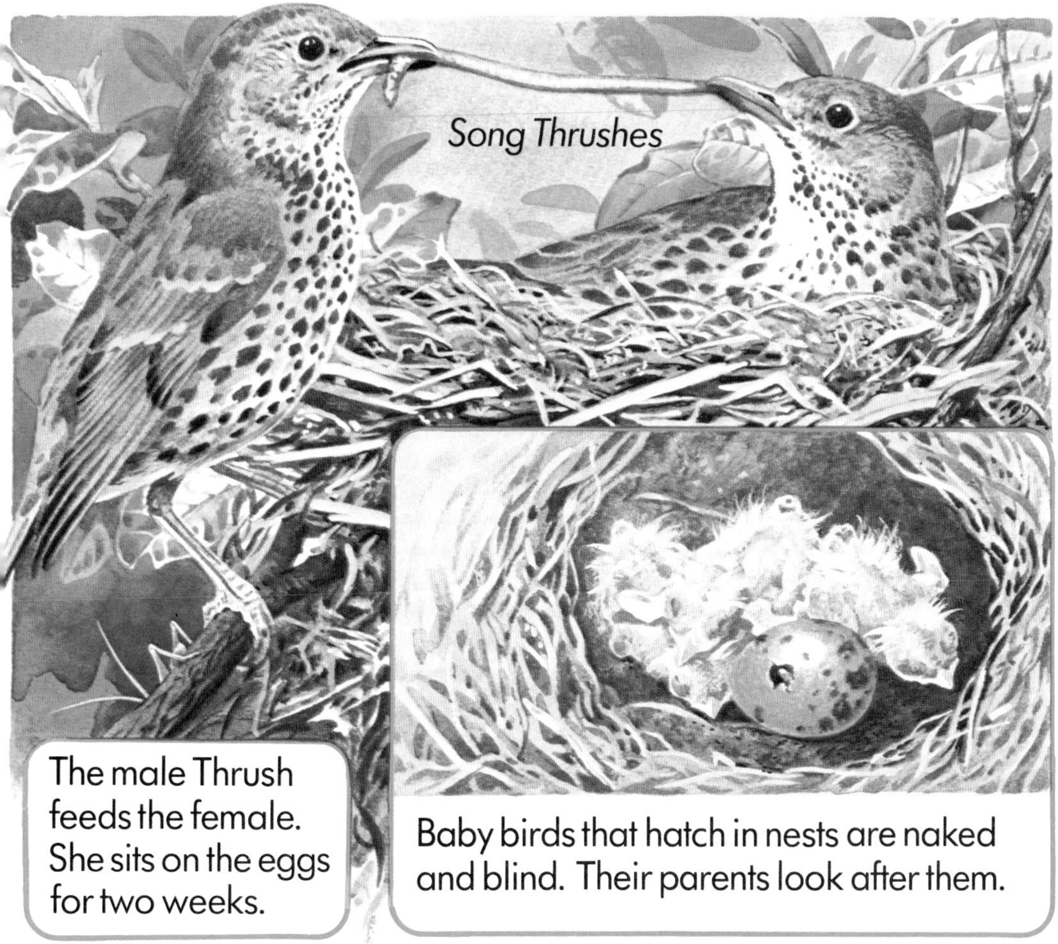

The male Thrush feeds the female. She sits on the eggs for two weeks.

Baby birds that hatch in nests are naked and blind. Their parents look after them.

Rock Warbler nest

Golden Oriole eggs

Hummingbird eggs

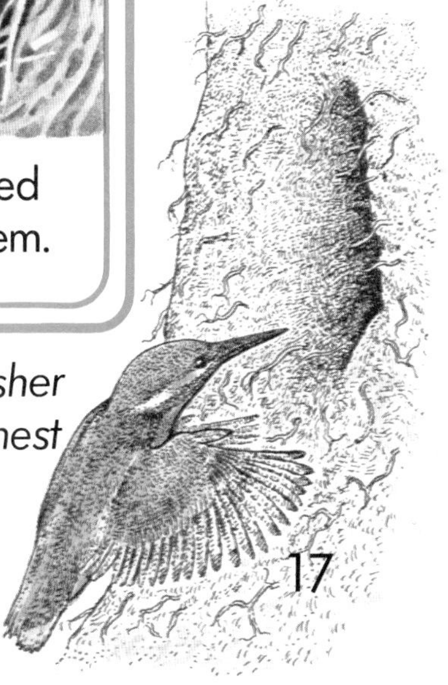

Kingfisher nest

Growing up

Thrushes collect food from their home area near the nest.

Baby Thrushes stay in the nest for two weeks until most of their feathers have grown.

Baby birds are always hungry. When their parents land on the nest, the baby birds open their beaks wide and call loudly. The bright colours inside their beaks make their parents feed them.

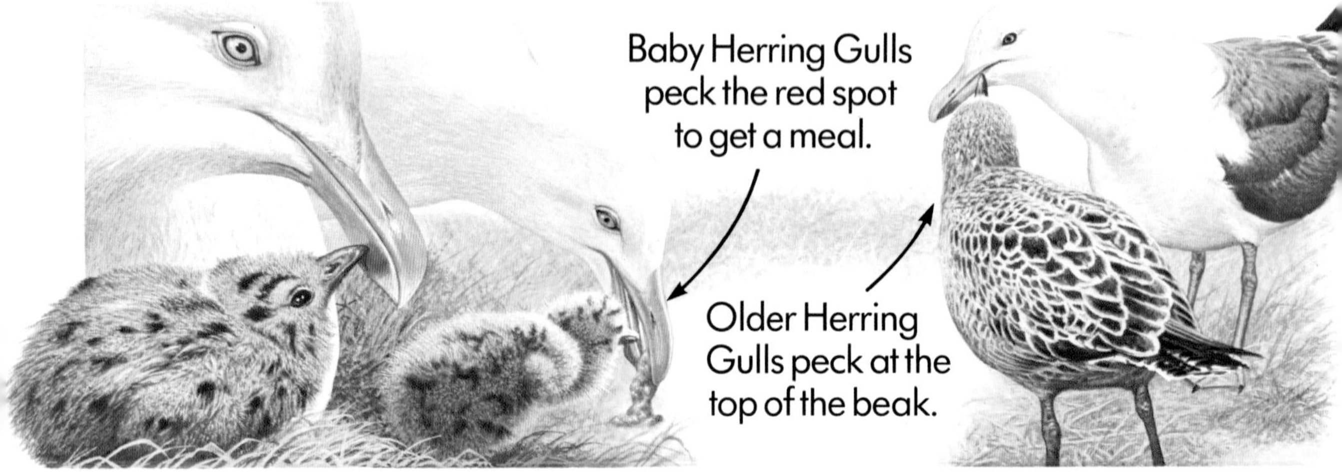

Baby Herring Gulls peck the red spot to get a meal.

Older Herring Gulls peck at the top of the beak.

Herring Gulls may have to fly far away to collect food for their babies. They swallow the food that they collect. When they get back, they cough up the food for the babies to eat.

Baby geese may watch their parents to find out what to eat.

They may sit on their mother's back if they are cold or tired.

A short time after they hatch, baby geese can swim. They will go into the water to escape from enemies.

Young geese take about six weeks to grow all their feathers. They can now fly, but they may practise twisting and turning in the air. They may also practise taking off and landing.

Resting and preening

At night most birds find a safe place to rest. They do not like flying at night because they cannot see well in the dark.

Hundreds of Starlings often fly to the same place every evening. They all rest together for the night.

Some birds tuck their beaks under their wings when they sleep. They fluff out their feathers to keep themselves warm.

Birds don't fall out of trees when they sleep. This is because when they bend their legs, their toes lock on to the branch.

Lots of Wrens may sleep together to keep warm.

All birds clean and tidy up their feathers. This is called preening. Most birds also spread oil on their feathers to keep them in good condition.

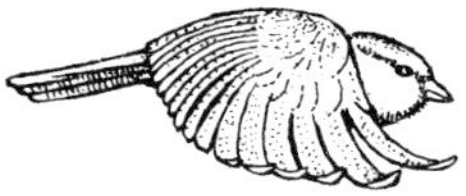

Birds squeeze oil out of a gland just above the tail.

Some birds preen each other.

Some birds have a bath.

Birds that do not fly

The Ostrich is the largest bird in the world. It is too heavy to fly and it has only small wing feathers. The Ostrich cannot fly away from enemies, but it can look after itself in other ways.

It is taller than a man. It can see enemies a long way away.
The beak of an Ostrich is strong enough to crack the skull of an enemy.
The Ostrich has long legs with strong muscles. It can run faster than its enemies.
On its big toe, it has a dangerous claw. It could kick an enemy to death.
big toe

Penguins do not fly with their wings. Do you know how they use them?

Penguins use their wings as flippers. They can swim very fast on top of the water or under the water.

Penguins use their wings to help them balance.

These Penguins are hunting for fish.

Penguins use their wings and their beaks when they quarrel.

Penguins can jump out of the sea.

Rockhopper Penguins

Picture puzzle

There are 13 birds hidden in this picture.
Can you find them all?

TREES

Games

1. Hunt the Nut Weevil

Nut Weevils live on trees. Can you find 10 more Nut Weevils in the tree pages ?

2. Watch the leaf bud open

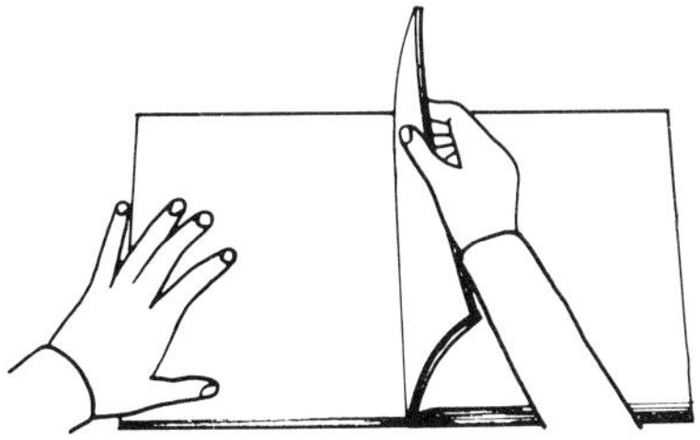

Hold the Tree pages like this.

Watch the top right hand corner and flick the pages over fast.

Amazing facts about trees

Trees are the largest plants in the world. They also live the longest.

On a warm day in spring, a large tree like this takes up 250 gallons of water from the soil. The water would fill five baths.

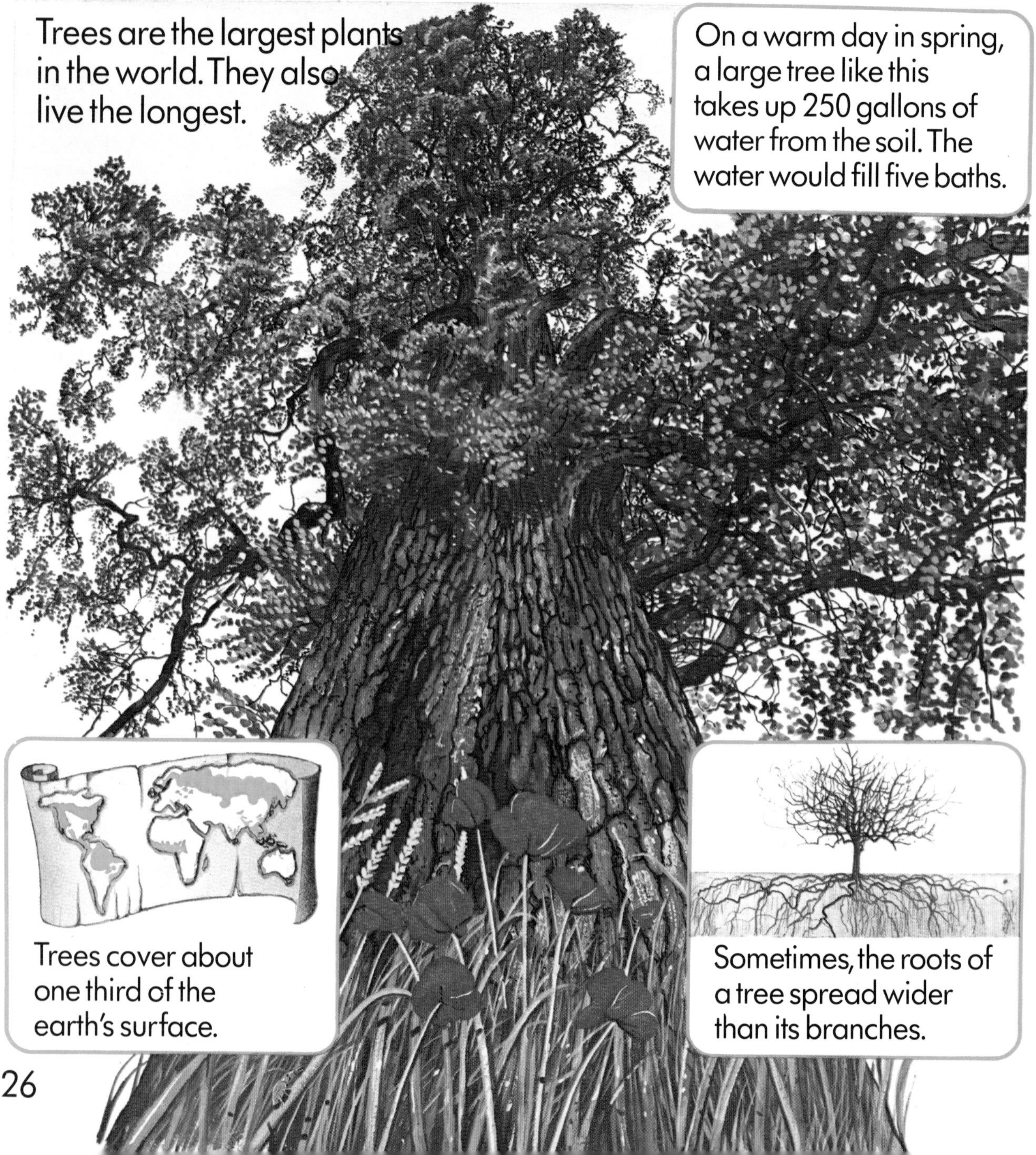

Trees cover about one third of the earth's surface.

Sometimes, the roots of a tree spread wider than its branches.

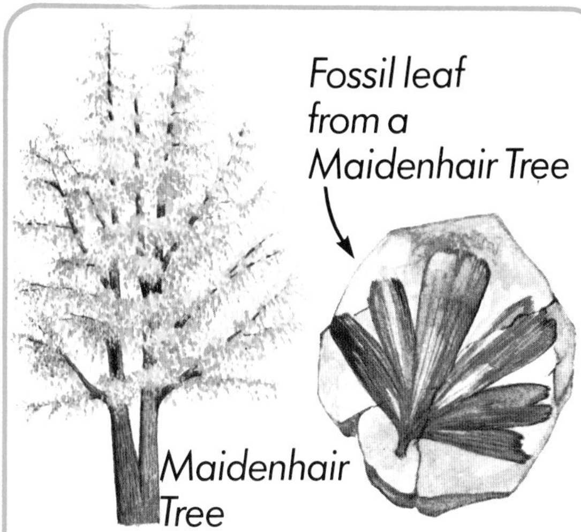

Maidenhair trees today look almost the same as ones that grew 200 million years ago.

This tree has been alive for 4,900 years.
It grows in America.

People say that this tree has enough wood to make all these bungalows.
It is the biggest tree in the world.
It is 83 metres tall and 24 metres round the trunk.

This Sierra Redwood tree grows in California, in North America.

Trees in the countryside

This picture shows you some of the places where trees grow. Some of them grow naturally and some are planted by people.

This is a windy hillside. The branches of the trees grow bent over because of the wind.
Trees in a wood grow close together. They have thin trunks and not very many lower branches.
People sometimes plant trees around their houses to protect them from wind and frost.
A tree growing on its own has spreading branches.
Some trees grow near water.

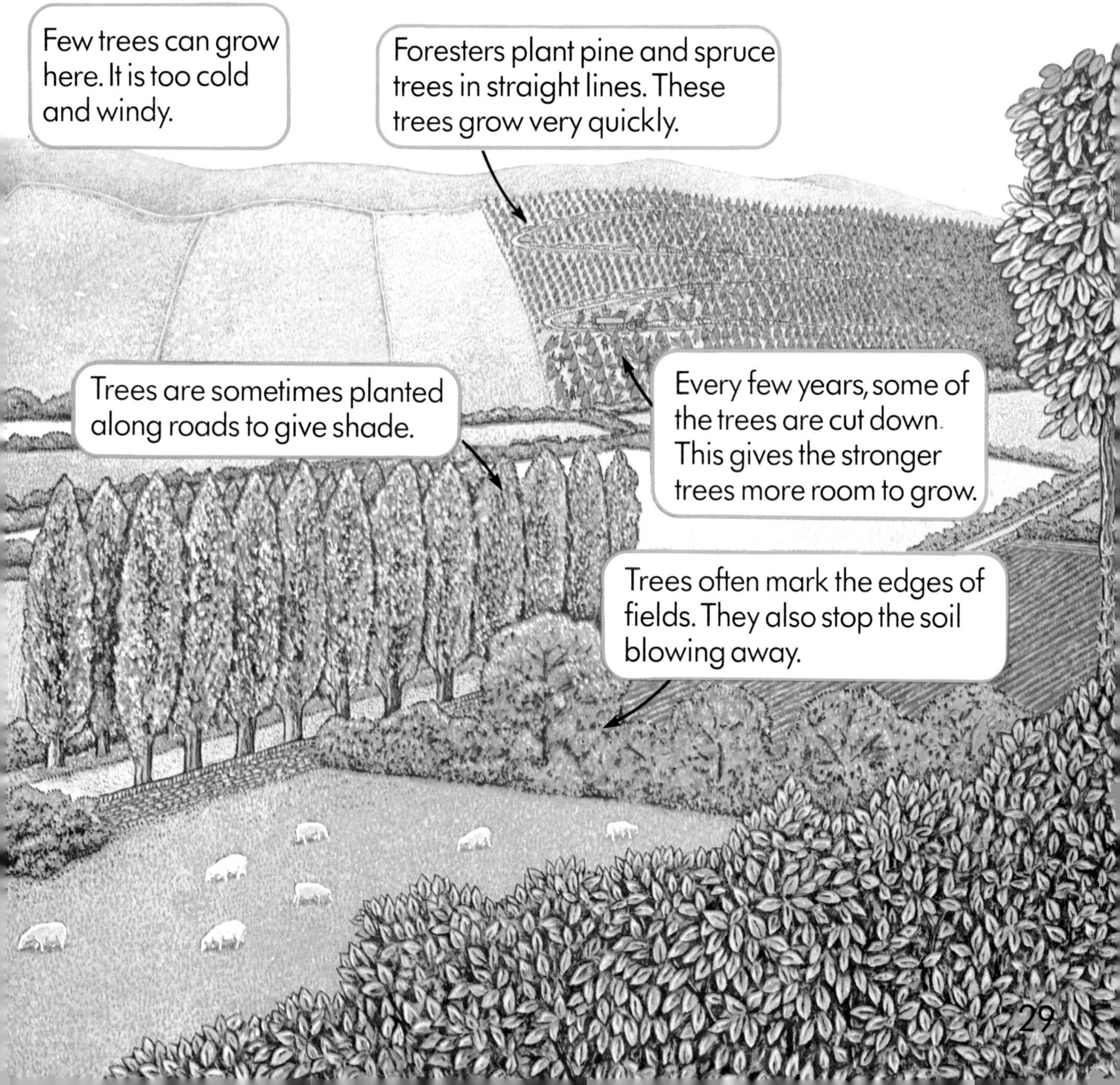
Few trees can grow here. It is too cold and windy.
Foresters plant pine and spruce trees in straight lines. These trees grow very quickly.
Trees are sometimes planted along roads to give shade.
Every few years, some of the trees are cut down. This gives the stronger trees more room to grow.
Trees often mark the edges of fields. They also stop the soil blowing away.

Under the ground

Roots help a tree in many ways. They take up water and minerals from the soil. A tree needs these to grow. They hold the tree in place and they also hold the soil together. On steep ground, they help stop the soil from washing away in the rain.

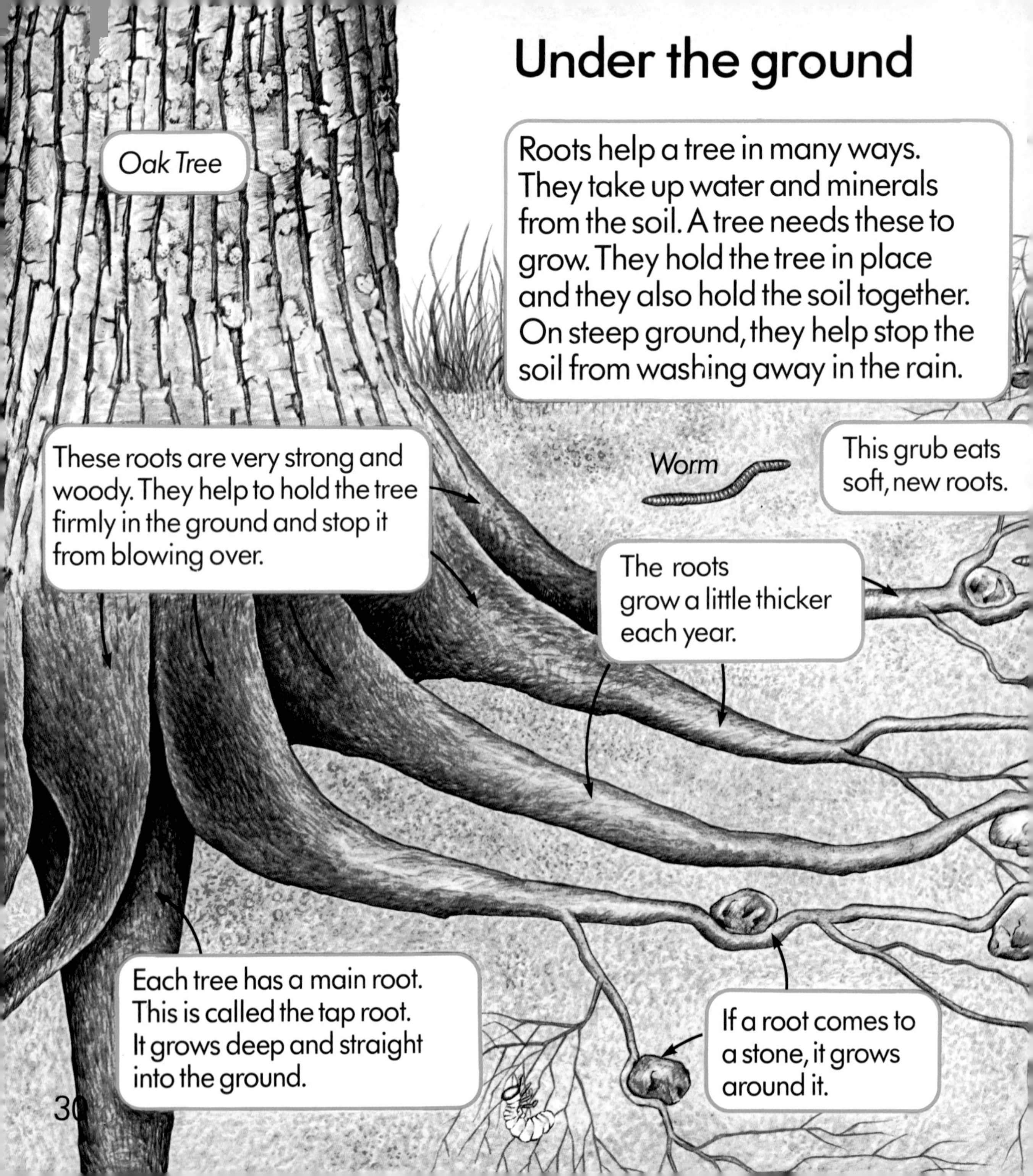

Oak Tree
These roots are very strong and woody. They help to hold the tree firmly in the ground and stop it from blowing over.
Worm
This grub eats soft, new roots.
The roots grow a little thicker each year.
Each tree has a main root. This is called the tap root. It grows deep and straight into the ground.
If a root comes to a stone, it grows around it.

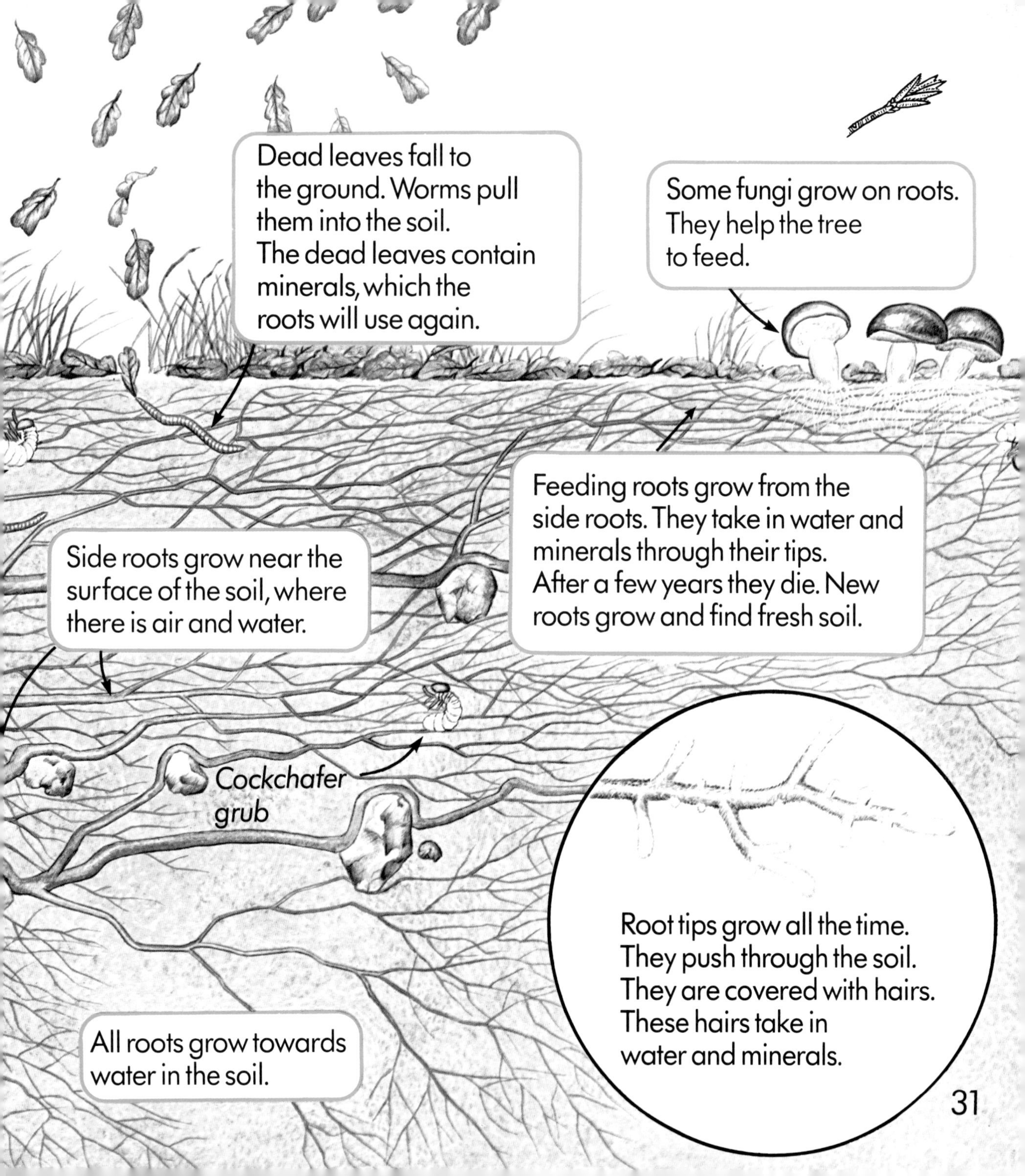
Dead leaves fall to the ground. Worms pull them into the soil. The dead leaves contain minerals, which the roots will use again.
Some fungi grow on roots. They help the tree to feed.
Feeding roots grow from the side roots. They take in water and minerals through their tips. After a few years they die. New roots grow and find fresh soil.
Side roots grow near the surface of the soil, where there is air and water.
Cockchafer grub
Root tips grow all the time. They push through the soil. They are covered with hairs. These hairs take in water and minerals.
All roots grow towards water in the soil.

How a twig grows

This is how a Beech twig grows in one year.

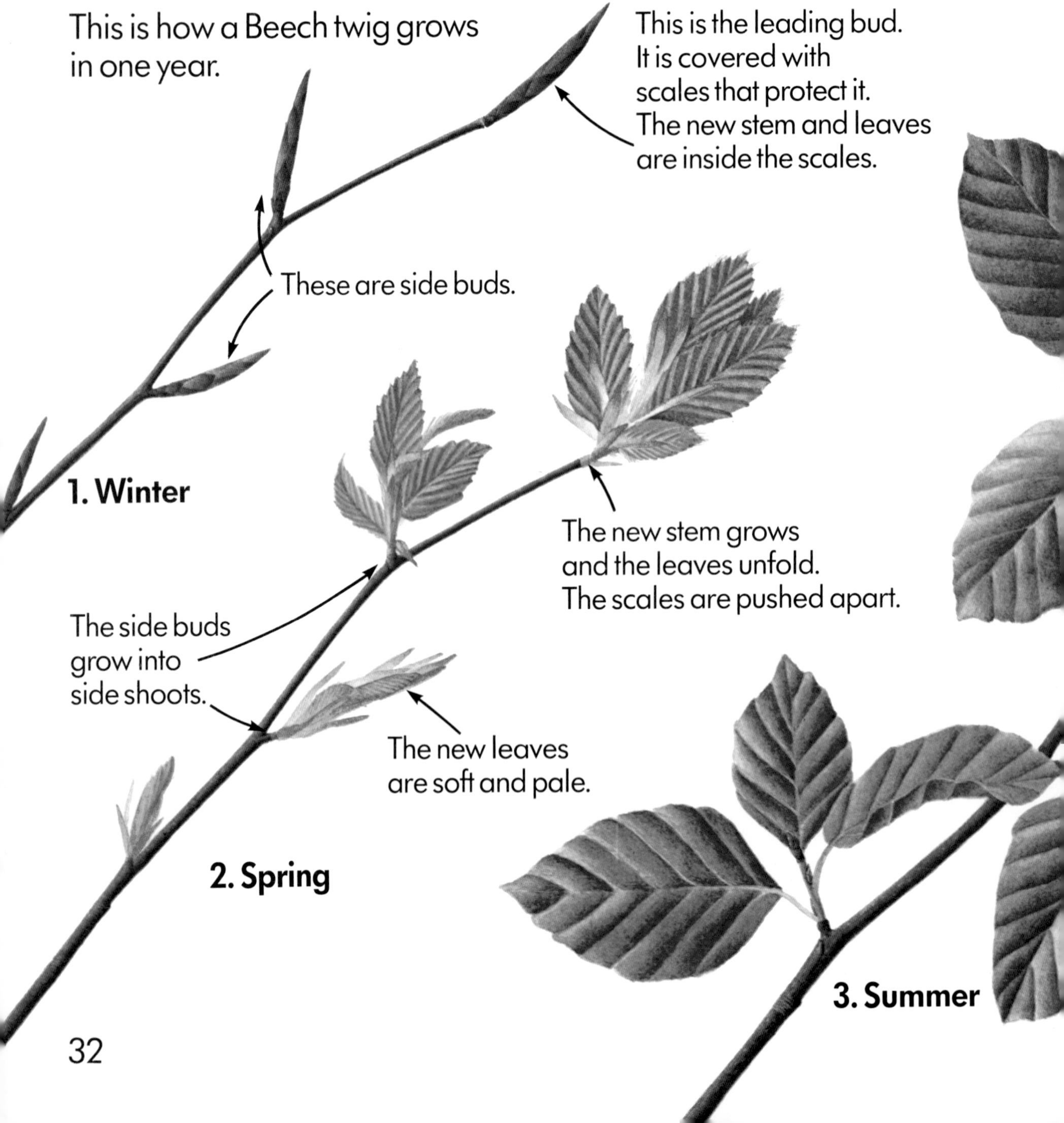

This is the leading bud. It is covered with scales that protect it. The new stem and leaves are inside the scales.
These are side buds.
1. Winter
The new stem grows and the leaves unfold. The scales are pushed apart.
The side buds grow into side shoots.
The new leaves are soft and pale.
2. Spring
3. Summer

By summer, the stems are stiff and the leaves are dark green and shiny.

When the twig stops growing, it makes a new leading bud. Next spring, this bud will grow into a new shoot.

Towards the end of summer, a new bud is made just above each leaf stalk. Next year, this bud will grow into a new side shoot.

The leaves turn brown before they fall off.

This is where the leading bud was in the winter. The bud scales have left a scar. It is called a girdle scar. If you count the girdle scars on a twig, you can find out how old the twig is. This twig is two years old.

4. Autumn

Tree stumps

This is the inside of a healthy tree stump.

Most of the inside is sapwood. This carries water and minerals up from the roots to the leaves.

A very thin layer under the bark makes a new ring of sapwood every year.

In the middle is the heartwood. It is old, dead sapwood. It is very hard and strong.

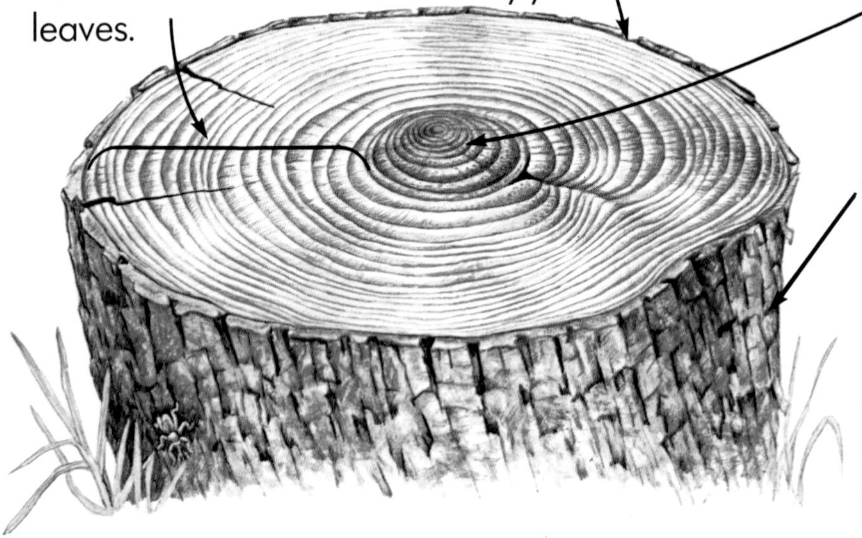

Bark stops the tree from drying out and protects it from insects and disease. Bark cannot stretch. It splits or peels as the wood inside grows. New bark grows underneath.

This is how a tree may die.

spores

Fungus spores in the air get into a wound in the tree.

The fungus spreads inside the trunk. The heartwood rots.

The heartwood in this tree is rotten.

Once the tree gets weak inside, it falls over in a storm.

When a tree dies, the bark becomes loose. Animals and plants can get under the bark. Many of them feed on the rotting wood.

Bracket Fungi grow on the trunk and feed on the rotting wood.
Slugs eat dead leaves and fungi. In dry weather they hide in cracks under the bark.
Longhorn Beetle
Scarlet Cup Fungi
Bark Beetles and their grubs make long tunnels under the bark.
Centipedes live under the bark. They come out at night to hunt for small insects.
Woodlice hide in damp places under the bark. They feed on rotting wood.
Millipedes live on the ground. They feed on dead leaves.

Deciduous tree leaves

Many trees are deciduous. This means that they lose their leaves in autumn. Most deciduous trees have soft, flat leaves.

Rowan

Oak

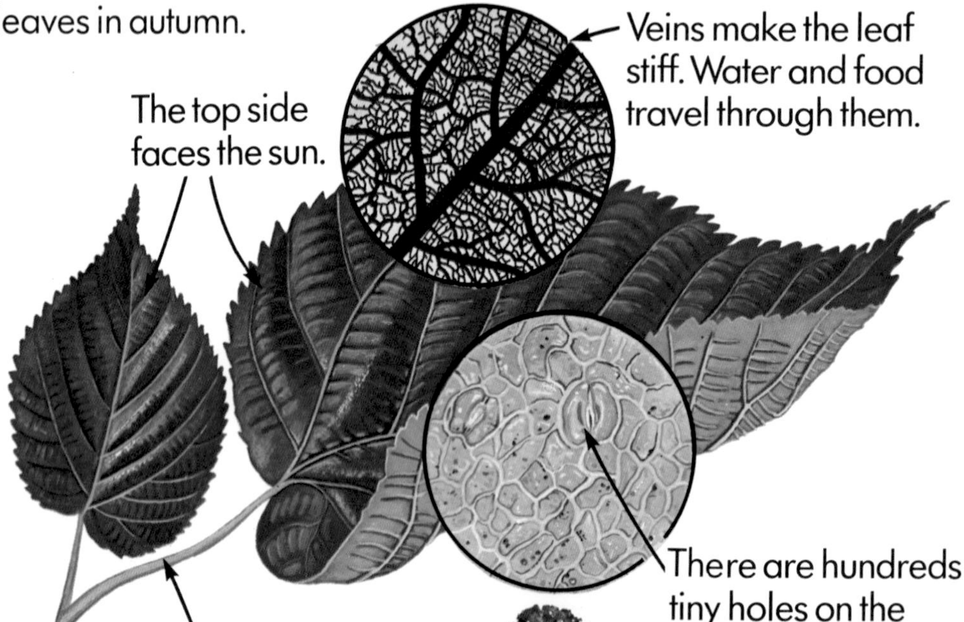
Lime trees lose their leaves in autumn.
Veins make the leaf stiff. Water and food travel through them.
The top side faces the sun.
There are hundreds of tiny holes on the underside. These open and close to let air in and out and water out.
The leaf stalk can bend so that the leaf does not break on windy days. Water and food travel through it.

Lime

Sycamore

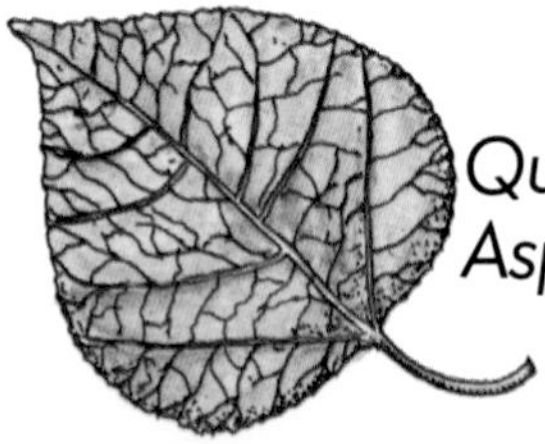

Quaking Aspen

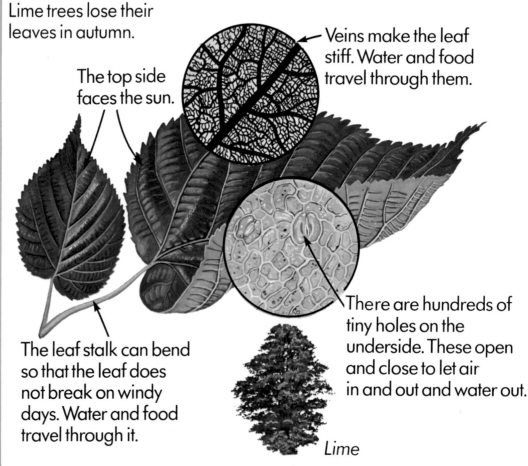

Horse Chestnut

Evergreen tree leaves

Other trees are called evergreens. They keep their leaves all winter. Most evergreens have tough, waxy leaves.

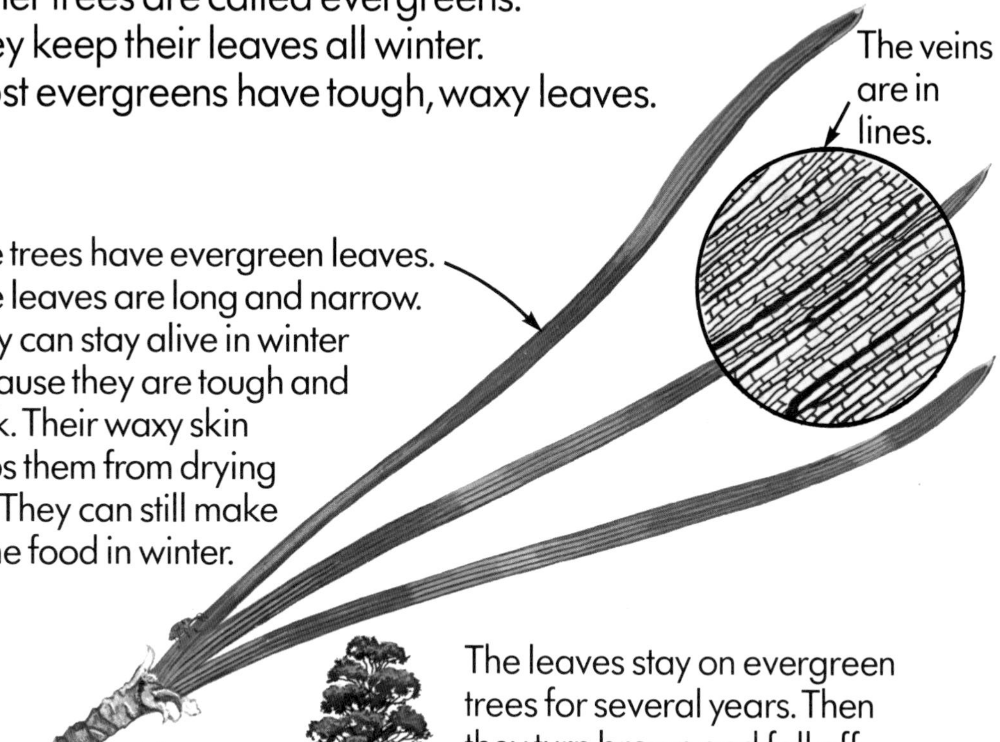
The veins are in lines.

Pine trees have evergreen leaves. Pine leaves are long and narrow. They can stay alive in winter because they are tough and thick. Their waxy skin stops them from drying out. They can still make some food in winter.

Monterey Pine

The leaves stay on evergreen trees for several years. Then they turn brown and fall off. They do not fall off all at once, so the tree always has some leaves.

Italian Cypress

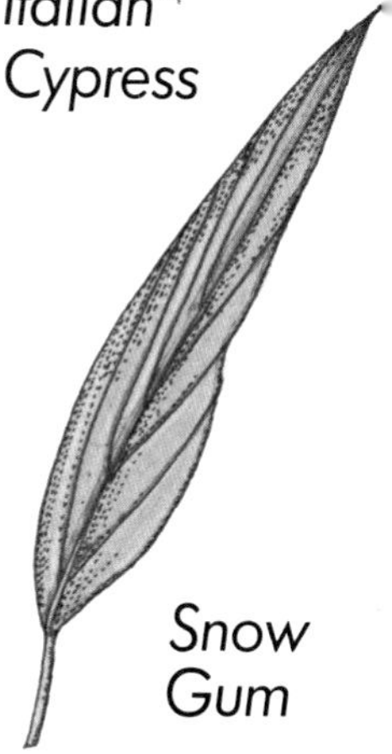

Snow Gum

Leaves are many different shapes, but they all do the same work. Turn over the page to see what they do.

lorway pruce

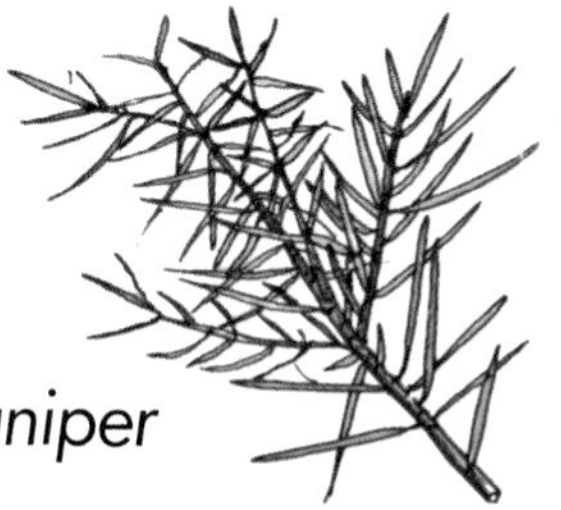

Juniper

Evergreen Oak

Scots Pine

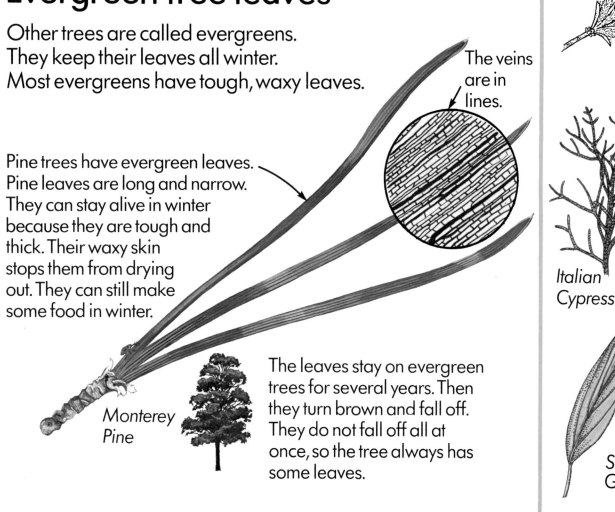

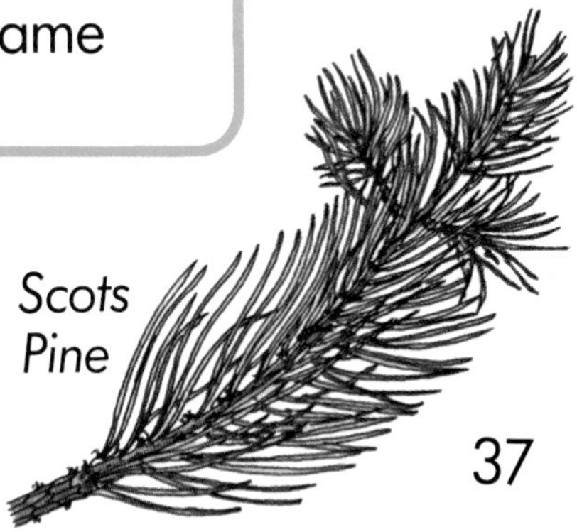

What leaves do

A tree breathes and feeds with its leaves.
Follow the numbers to see how a tree makes its food.

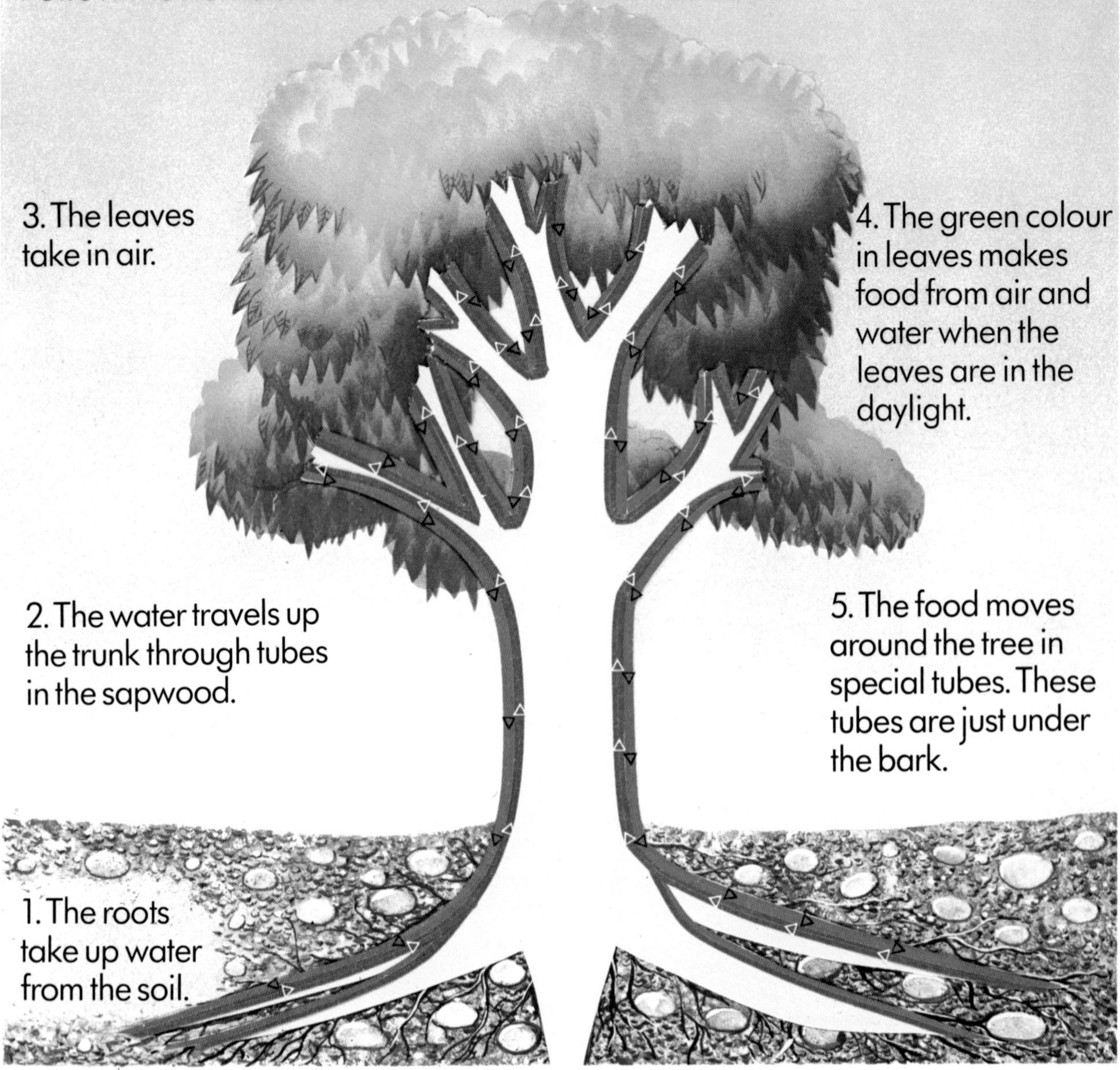

1. The roots take up water from the soil.
2. The water travels up the trunk through tubes in the sapwood.
3. The leaves take in air.
4. The green colour in leaves makes food from air and water when the leaves are in the daylight.
5. The food moves around the tree in special tubes. These tubes are just under the bark.

Why do deciduous trees lose their leaves in autumn?

1. In autumn, it is not warm enough for leaves to make much food. Also, wind and cold weather would damage soft leaves.

The corky layer forms here.

2. A corky layer grows across the leaf stalk. Water cannot get to the leaf any more. The leaf changes colour.

This is the new leaf bud. Below it is the scar where the leaf was joined to the twig.

3. The leaf dries out and dies. The wind blows it off the tree.

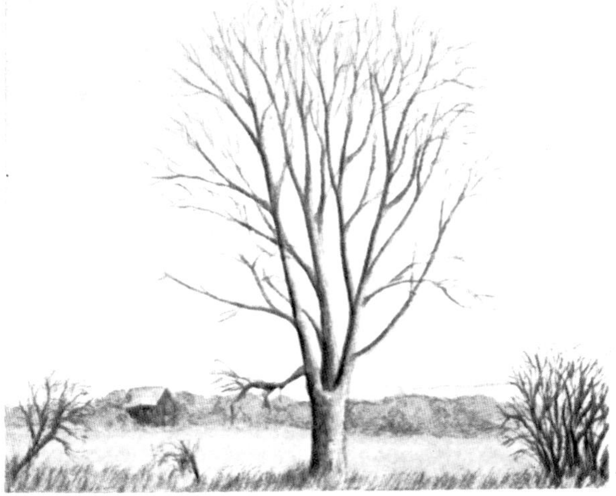

4. All the leaves fall off. The tree rests until spring.

Tree flowers

All trees have flowers. Flowers have stamens, which hold pollen, and a pistil, which holds ovules. Pollen that lands on the top of the pistil grows down to join with the ovules. This is called fertilization. Fertilized ovules grow into seeds.

1. The petals and sweet scent attract insects. The insects feed on a sweet liquid inside the flower. This is called nectar.

These are stamens. They make pollen.
Cherry Tree
Honeybee
This is the top of the pistil. It is called the stigma. Pollen sticks to it.

2. When an insect comes to feed, it brushes against the stamens. Pollen rubs on to its body.

3. When it visits a flower on another tree, the pollen is brushed on to the stigma. The flower can now make seeds.

Some trees have two kinds of flowers.
One kind has stamens.
The other kind has a pistil only.
The Alder Tree has stamen
flowers and pistil flowers
on the same twig.

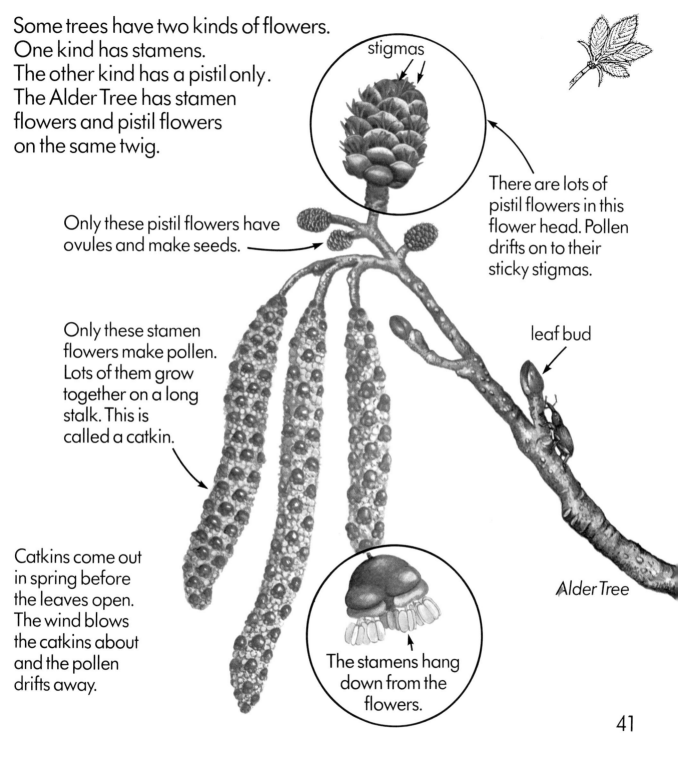

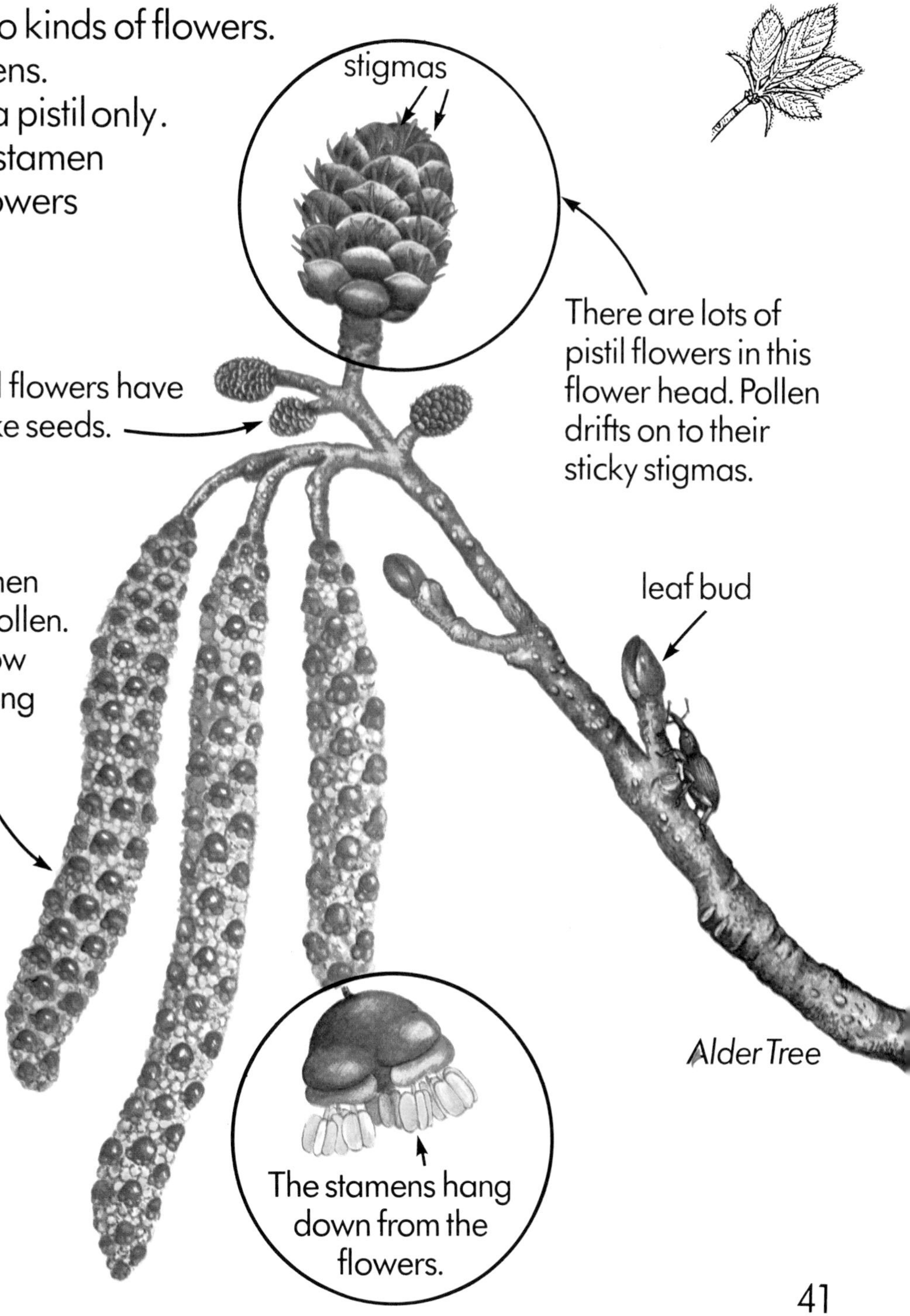

stigmas
There are lots of pistil flowers in this flower head. Pollen drifts on to their sticky stigmas.
Only these pistil flowers have ovules and make seeds.
Only these stamen flowers make pollen. Lots of them grow together on a long stalk. This is called a catkin.
leaf bud
The stamens hang down from the flowers.

Alder Tree

Catkins come out
in spring before
the leaves open.
The wind blows
the catkins about
and the pollen
drifts away.

Fruits and seeds

The fertilized ovules grow into seeds. Fruits grow to hold and protect them.

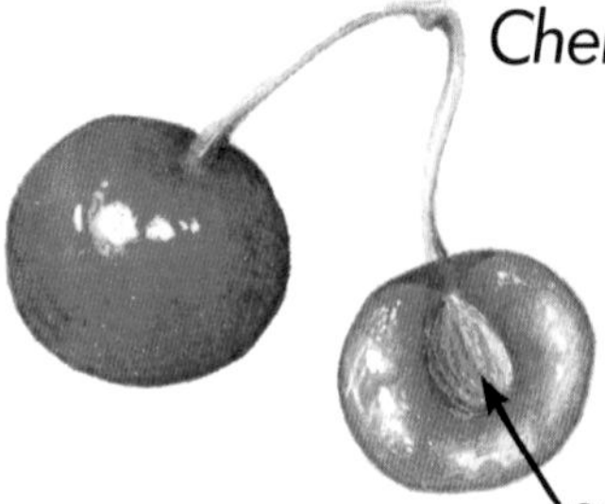

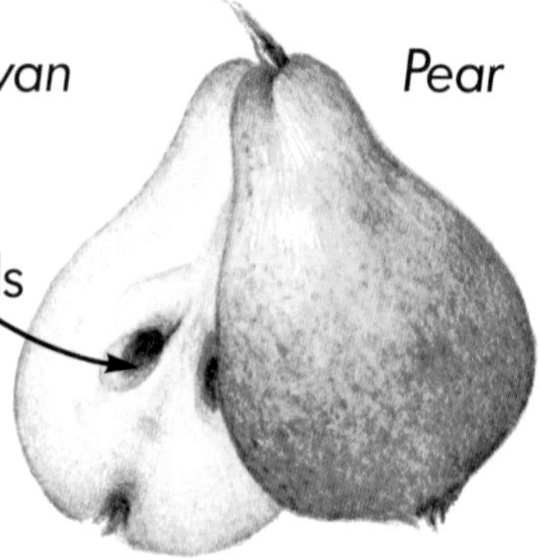

These fruits are soft and juicy. Birds and animals eat them. Some have only one seed inside, others have lots.

This fruit is spiky. It protects the seed inside.

This fruit is made of lots of seeds with feathery tops.

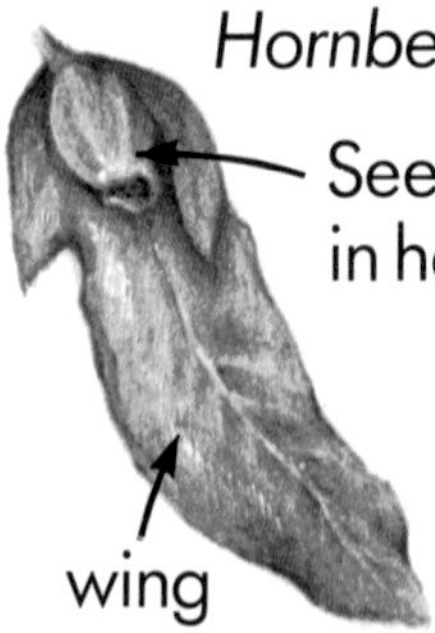

This fruit is hard and dry. It has a leafy wing.

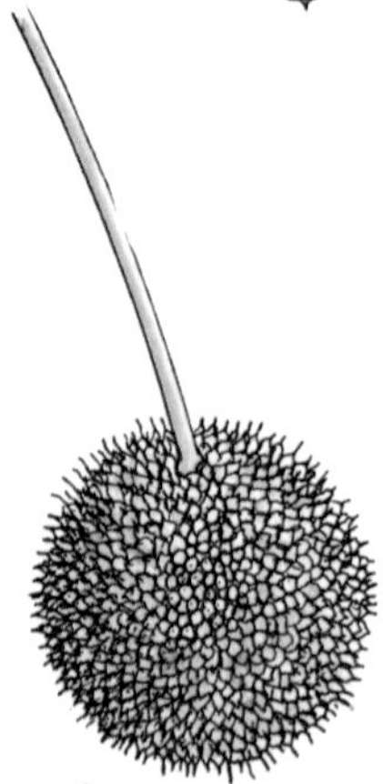

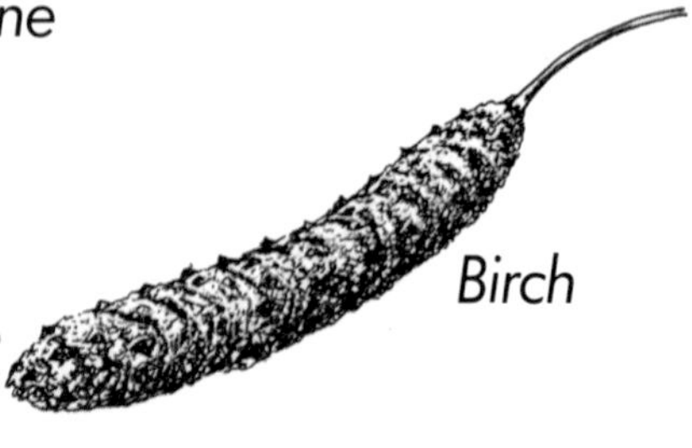

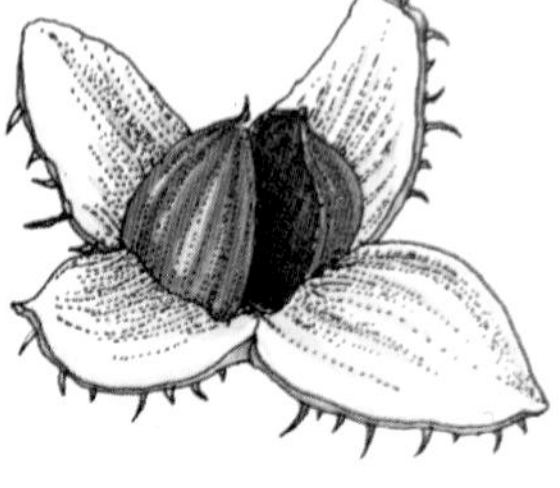

Many evergreen trees have fruits called cones. The flowers that grow at the tips of new shoots grow into cones. Sometimes this takes two years.

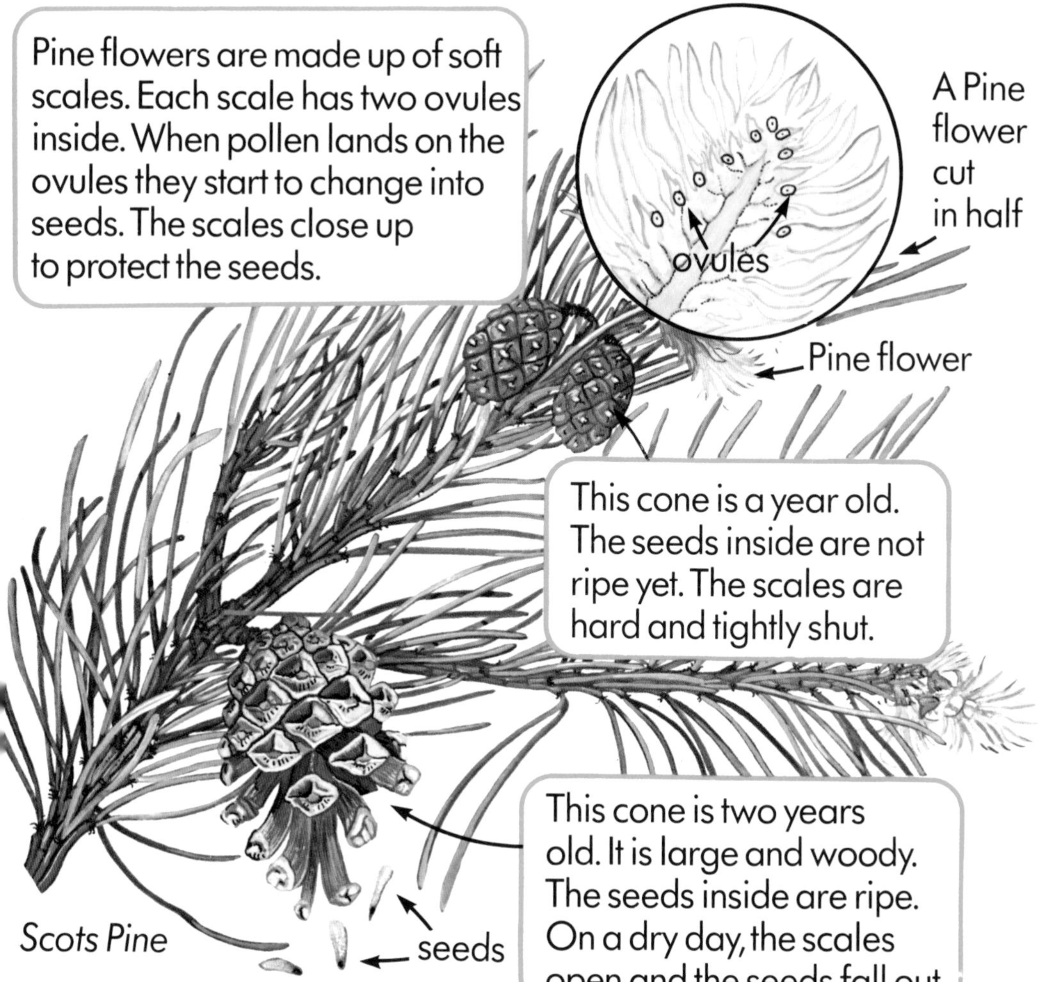

Pine flowers are made up of soft scales. Each scale has two ovules inside. When pollen lands on the ovules they start to change into seeds. The scales close up to protect the seeds.

This cone is a year old. The seeds inside are not ripe yet. The scales are hard and tightly shut.

This cone is two years old. It is large and woody. The seeds inside are ripe. On a dry day, the scales open and the seeds fall out.

Yew

Juniper

Crab Apple

Mulberry

Sweet Chestnut

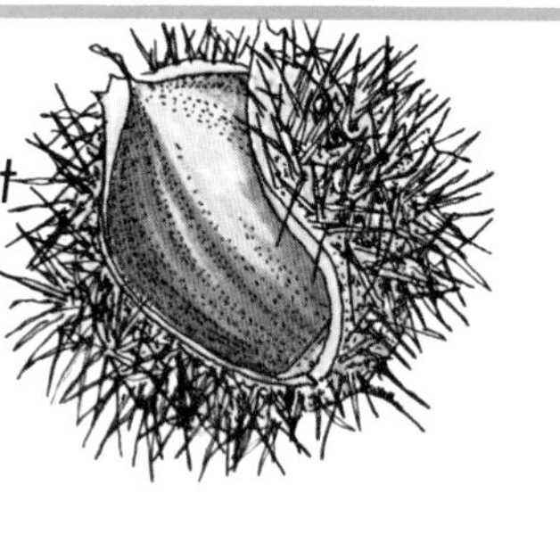

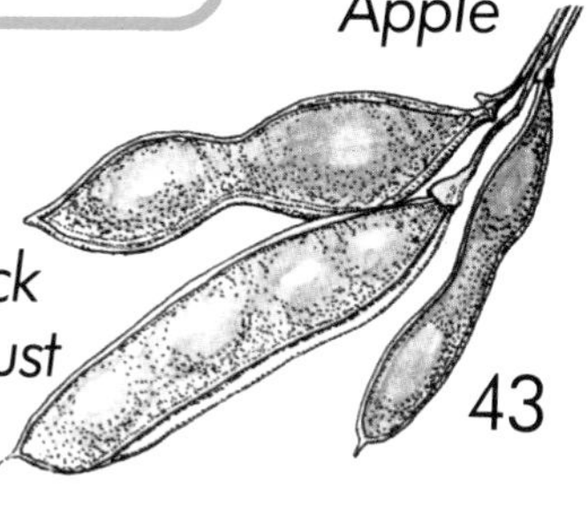

Black Locust

How seeds are moved

When the seeds in the fruits are ripe, the wind or animals may move them away from the tree. There is not enough light under the parent tree for the seedlings to grow well.

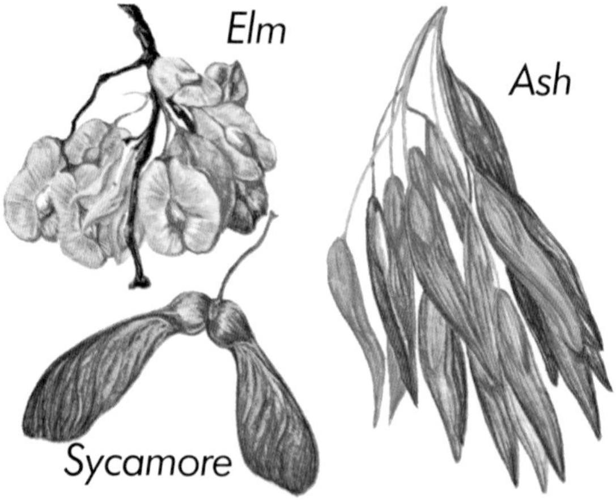

Fruits with wings spin away from the tree.

Some fruits are very light. They have tiny hairs that help them float away in the wind.

Squirrels carry acorns away from Oak Trees and bury them. Birds feed on acorns and drop some. A few of the acorns grow into trees.

Birds carry the fruits and seeds away from these trees. They eat the fruits and drop the seeds.

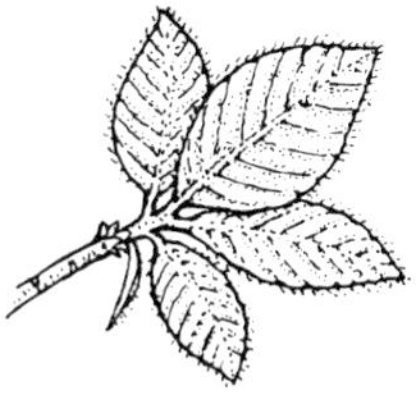

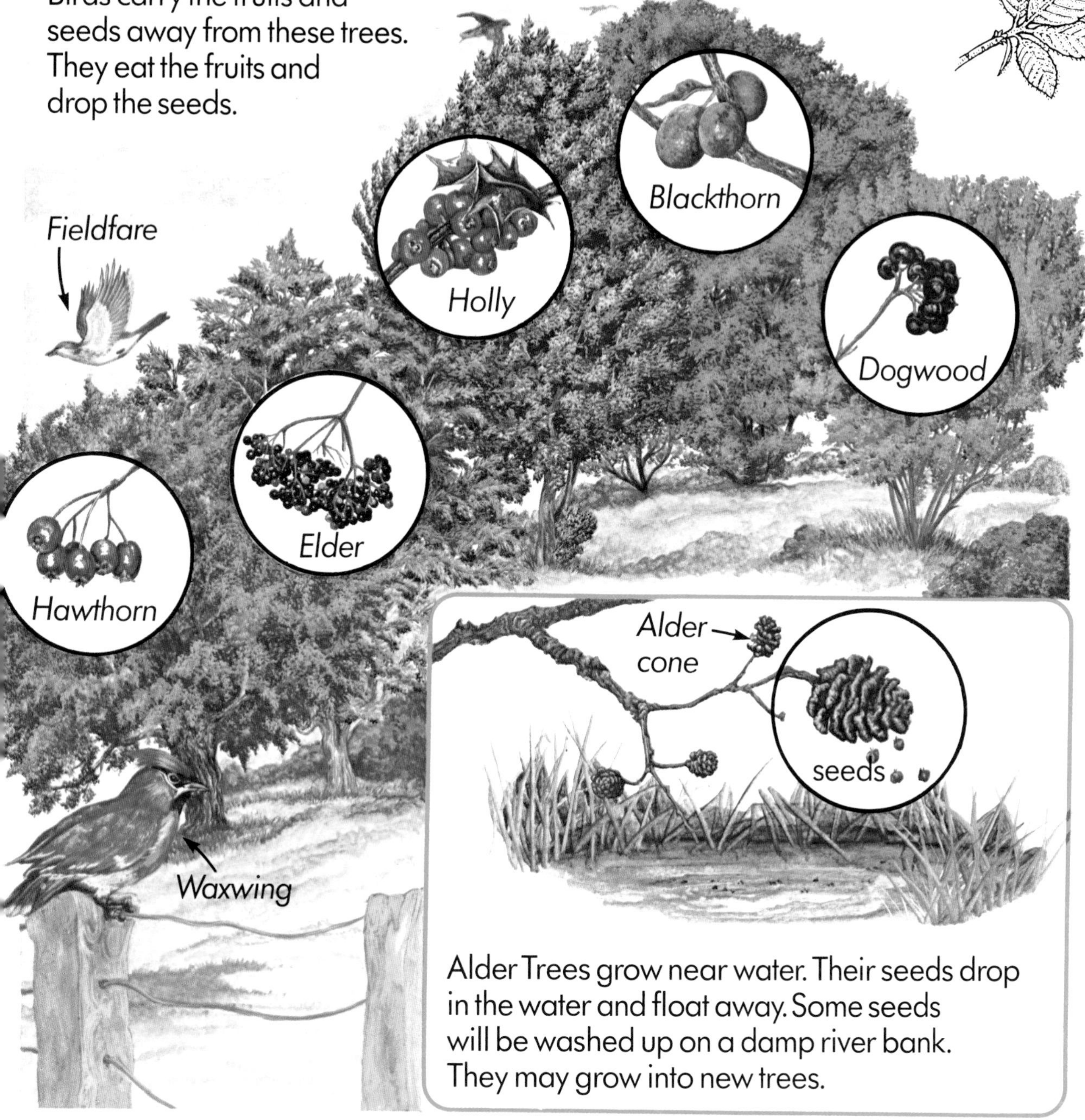

Alder Trees grow near water. Their seeds drop in the water and float away. Some seeds will be washed up on a damp river bank. They may grow into new trees.

Life on a tree

Keep a record book about a tree.
See how many insects live on the leaves or rest on the bark.
Watch how many birds visit it. Notice if any plants grow on it.

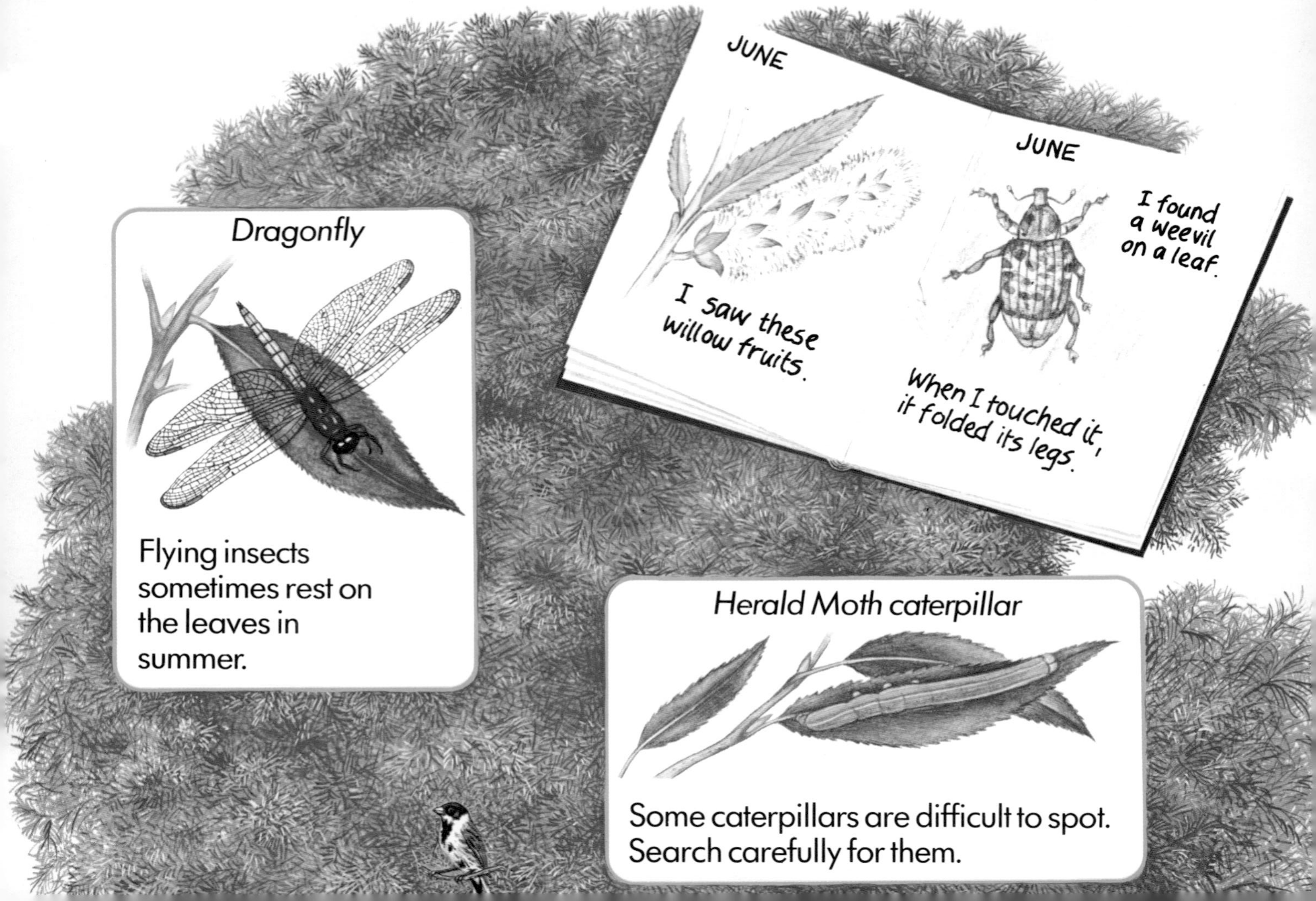

JUNE
I saw these willow fruits.
JUNE
I found a weevil on a leaf.
When I touched it, it folded its legs.

Dragonfly

Flying insects sometimes rest on the leaves in summer.

Herald Moth caterpillar

Some caterpillars are difficult to spot. Search carefully for them.

Leaf Beetle
Look for beetles on the leaves and flowers.
Willow fruits
Look for Willow fruits in spring and summer.
Birds often visit trees to nest or sleep. Some search for seeds or insects.
Poplar Hawk Moth
Red Underwing Moth
White Willow
Some moths rest on the trunk in the day. They fly at night.
These animals live on Willow trees.
Willow trees often grow in wet places.

Picture puzzle

People eat many things that grow on trees. They make many things from the wood. There are at least 20 things in this picture that come from trees. How many can you find?

FLOWERS

Games

1. Hunt the Bumblebee

Bumblebees visit flowers. Can you find 20 more Bumblebees in the flower pages?

2. Watch the flower open

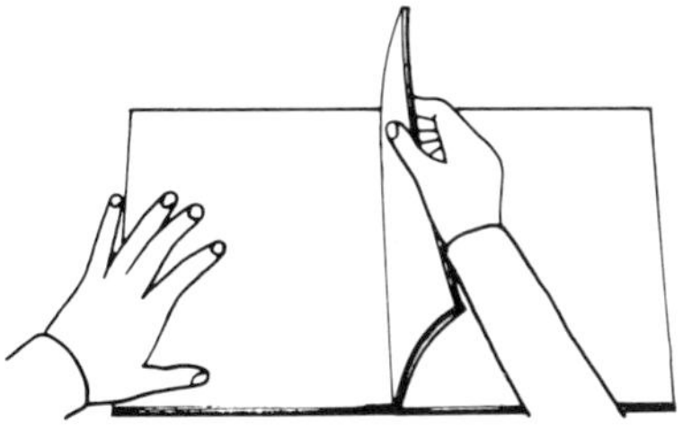

Hold the Flower pages like this.

Watch the top right hand corner and flick the pages over fast.

Looking at Buttercup flowers

If you look closely at a flower, you will see that it is made of lots of different parts.

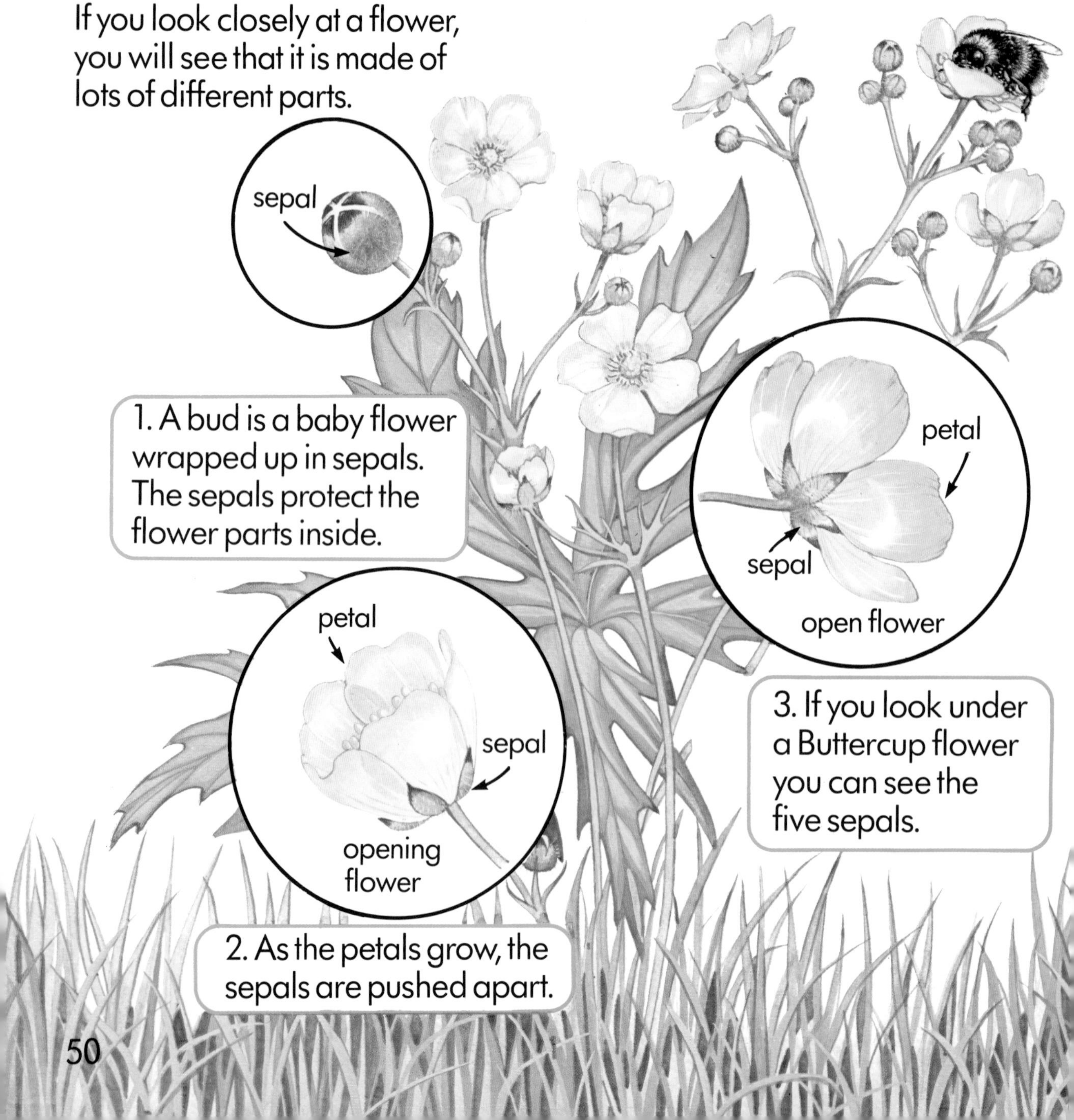

1. A bud is a baby flower wrapped up in sepals. The sepals protect the flower parts inside.

2. As the petals grow, the sepals are pushed apart.

3. If you look under a Buttercup flower you can see the five sepals.

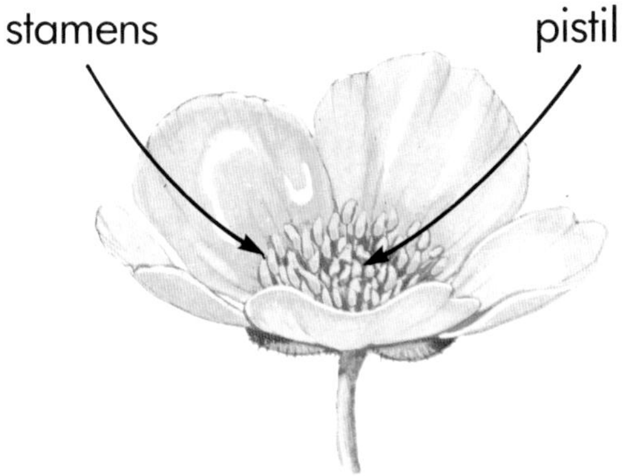

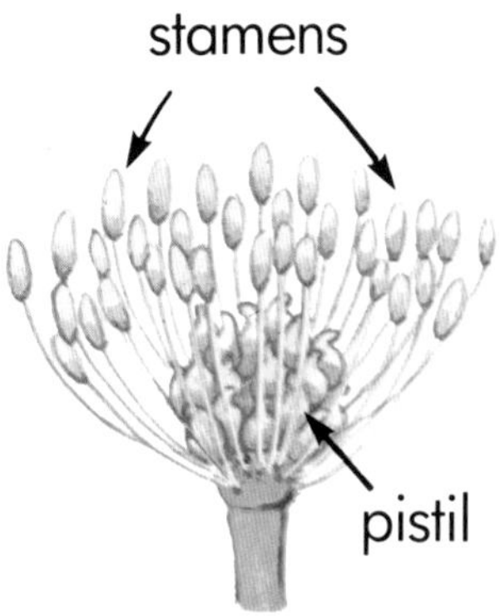

Inside the ring of petals are more flower parts. The green parts in the centre are called the pistil. Around it are stamens.

If you pull off the petals and sepals, you can see all the parts inside.

Each part of the pistil has a sticky top called a stigma.

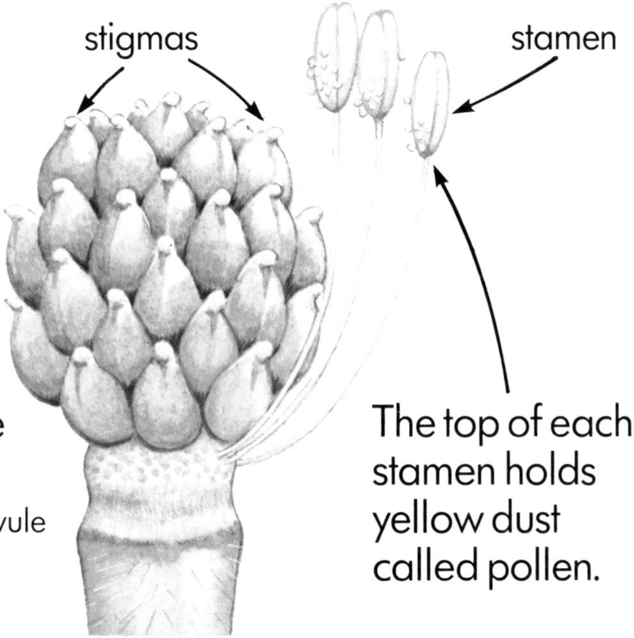

There is a tiny ovule inside each part of the pistil. It will grow into a seed.

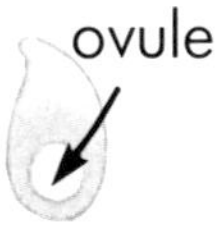

The top of each stamen holds yellow dust called pollen.

Looking at flower parts

Flower parts can be different shapes and sizes and different colours. You will have to look closely at each flower to see which part is which.

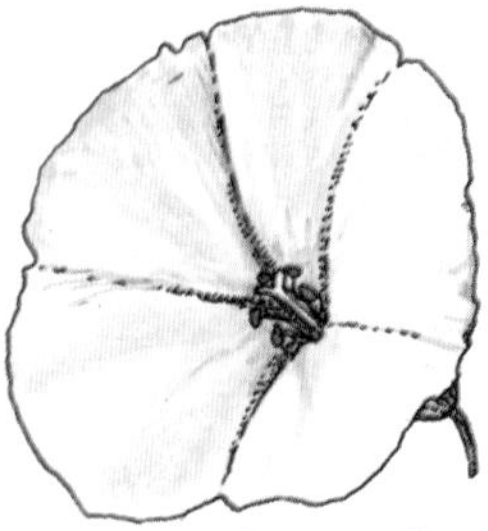

Bindweed

Lily

Pink

Some flowers have petals joined together.

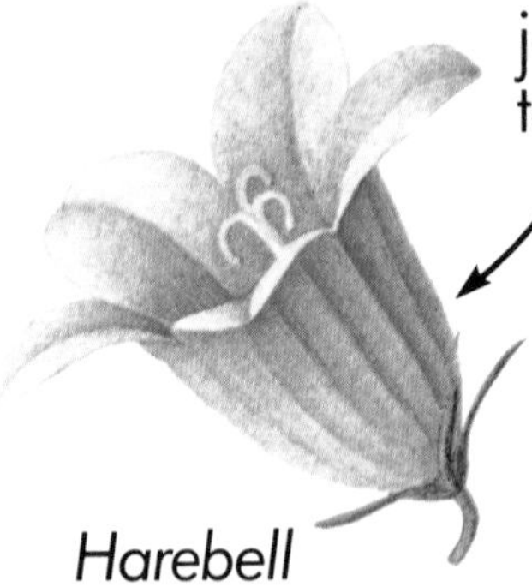

Harebell

Some have petals of different shapes and sizes.

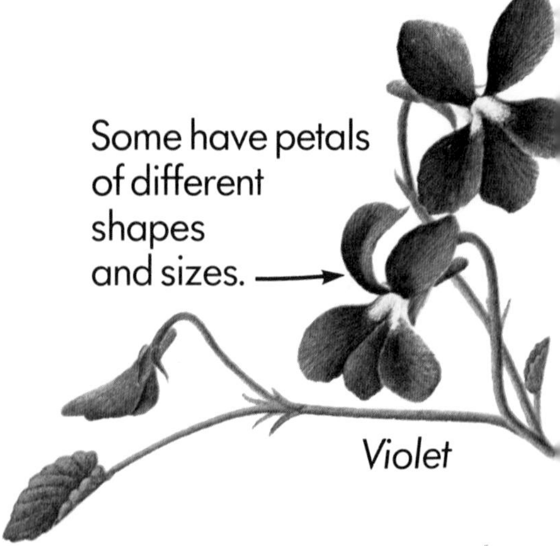

Violet

Some have lots of stamens.

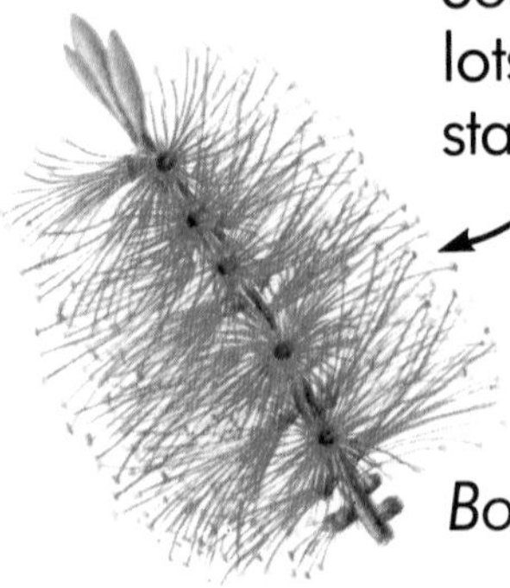

Bottlebrush

Some have brightly coloured sepals and brightly coloured petals.

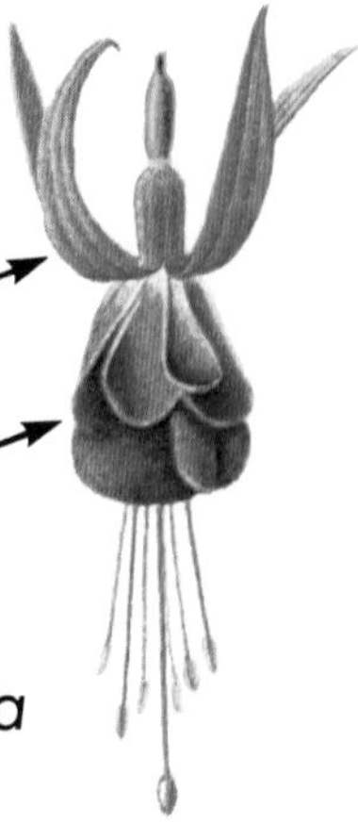

Fuchsia

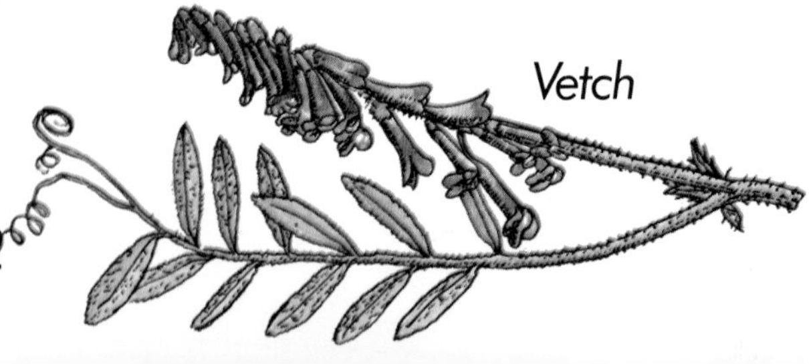

Vetch

Columbine

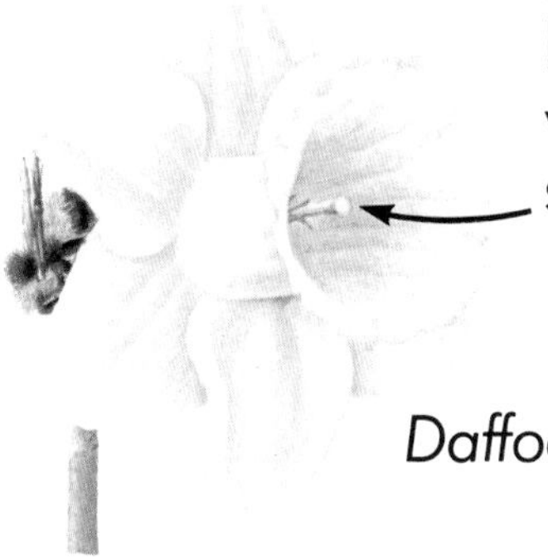

Daffodil

Some flowers have a pistil with only one stigma.

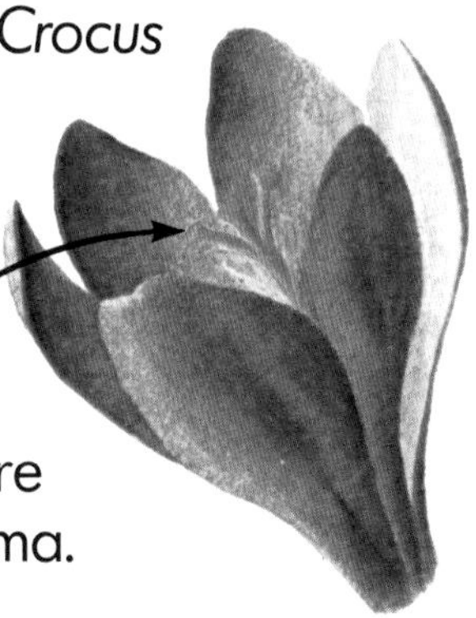

Crocus

Some have a pistil with more than one stigma.

Cranesbill

An Aster flower is made of lots of tiny flowers.

An Aster has tiny flowers on the outside with one long petal.

If you pull an Aster to bits, you can see the tiny yellow flowers on the inside.

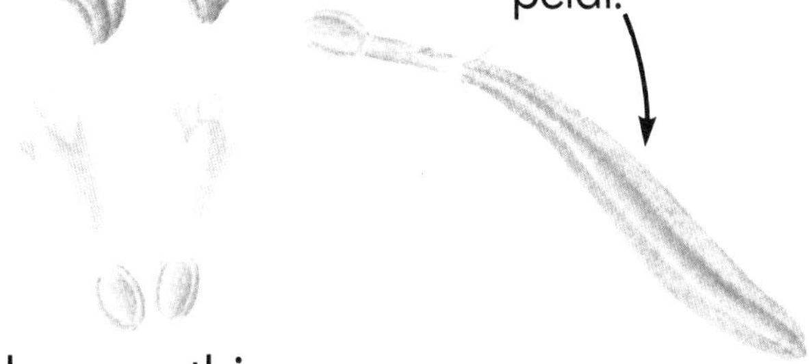

The Bumblebee is somewhere on this page.
Do you know why he visits flowers?
The answer is on the next page.

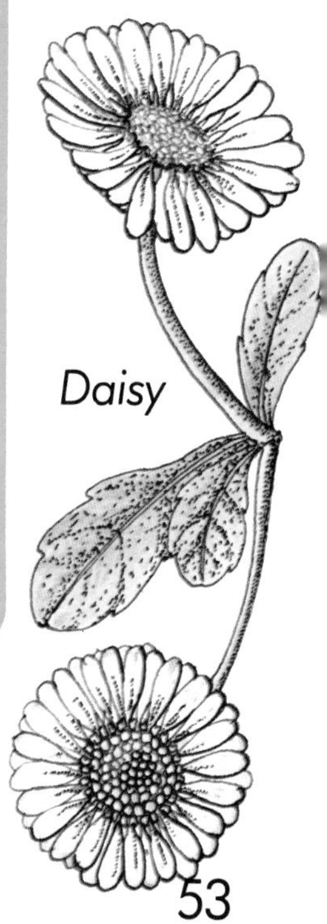

Daisy

Dandelion

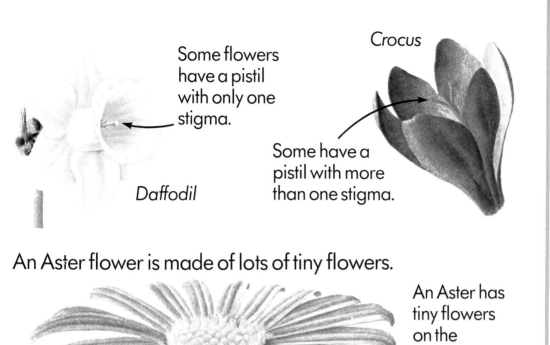

Dahlia

The visitors

Cranesbill

Flowers have many visitors. They are usually insects, such as bees. The Bumblebee visits flowers to drink a sweet liquid called nectar. Sometimes the visitors eat some of the pollen.

Many flowers have guide-lines or dots that point the way to the nectar.
Nectar is in here.

Yellow Flag

Visitors to this flower need long tongues to reach down to the nectar.

Most flowers have bright colours and a scent so visitors can find them. Butterflies like to visit pink, red and blue flowers.

Most moths drink nectar at night. They visit flowers that have a sweet scent. These flowers are easy to find in the dark.

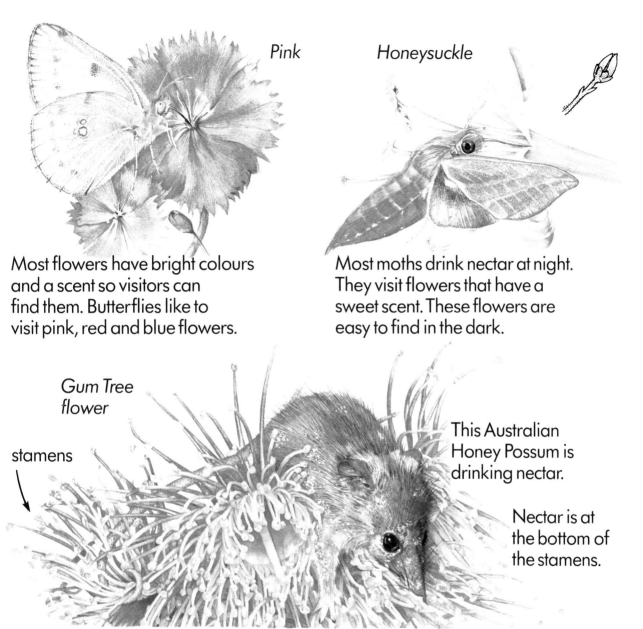

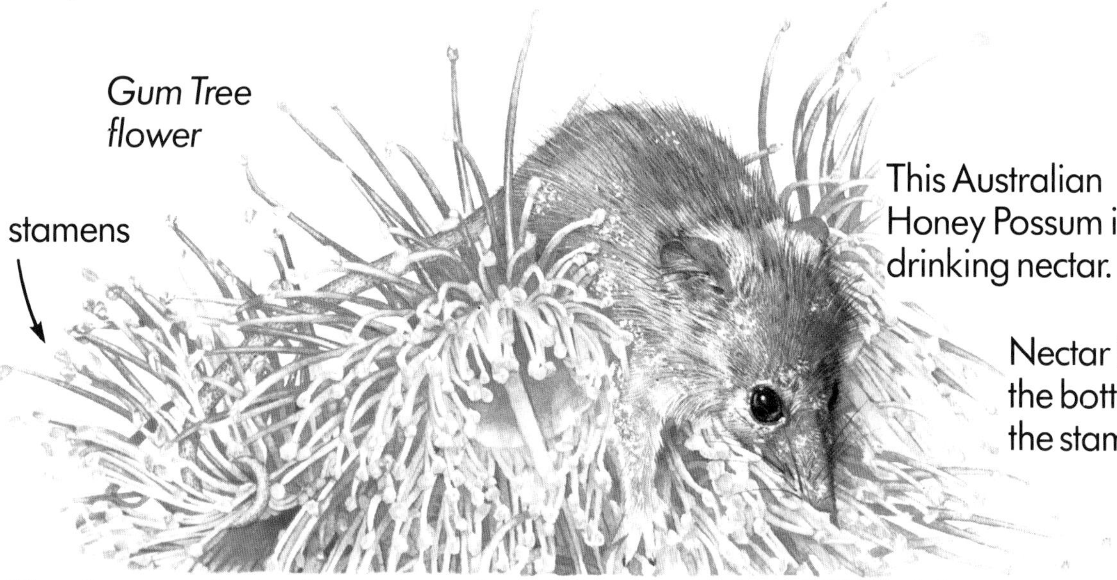

Gum Tree flower
stamens
This Australian Honey Possum is drinking nectar.
Nectar is at the bottom of the stamens.

The flowers help the visitors by giving them food. The visitors also help the flowers. Do you know what the visitors do? The answer is on the next page.

Why flowers need visitors

Visitors help plants by moving pollen from flower to flower.

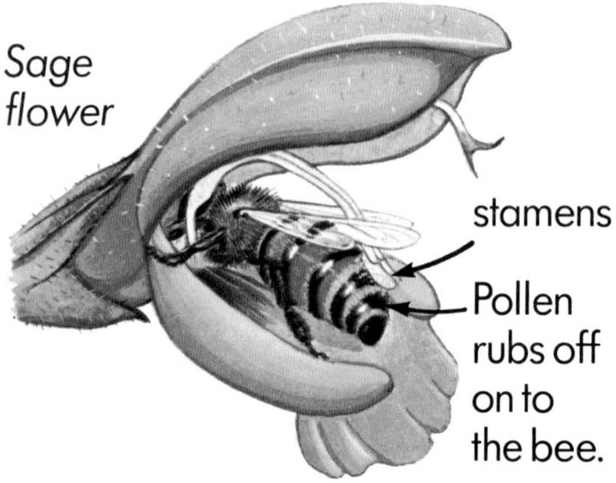

1. As a bee collects nectar from a flower, its body gets covered with pollen.

2. It flies to another Sage flower. It has pollen from the first flower on its back.

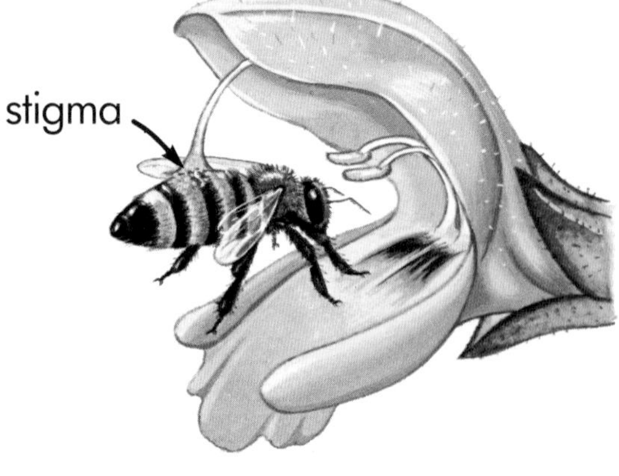

3. As it lands, the pollen on the bee's body rubs on to the stigma of the flower.

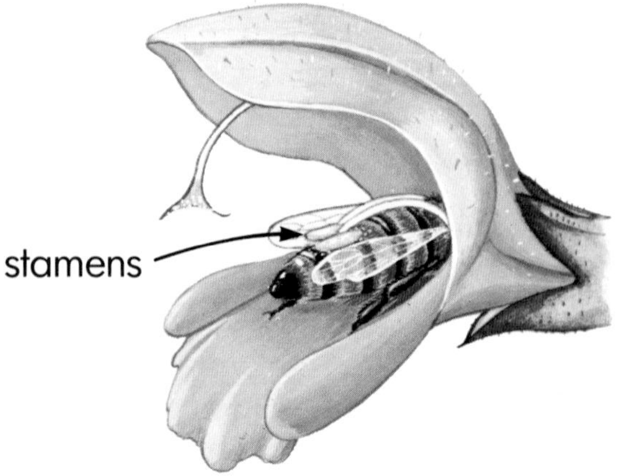

4. The bee goes into the flower. New pollen from the stamens rubs on to its back.

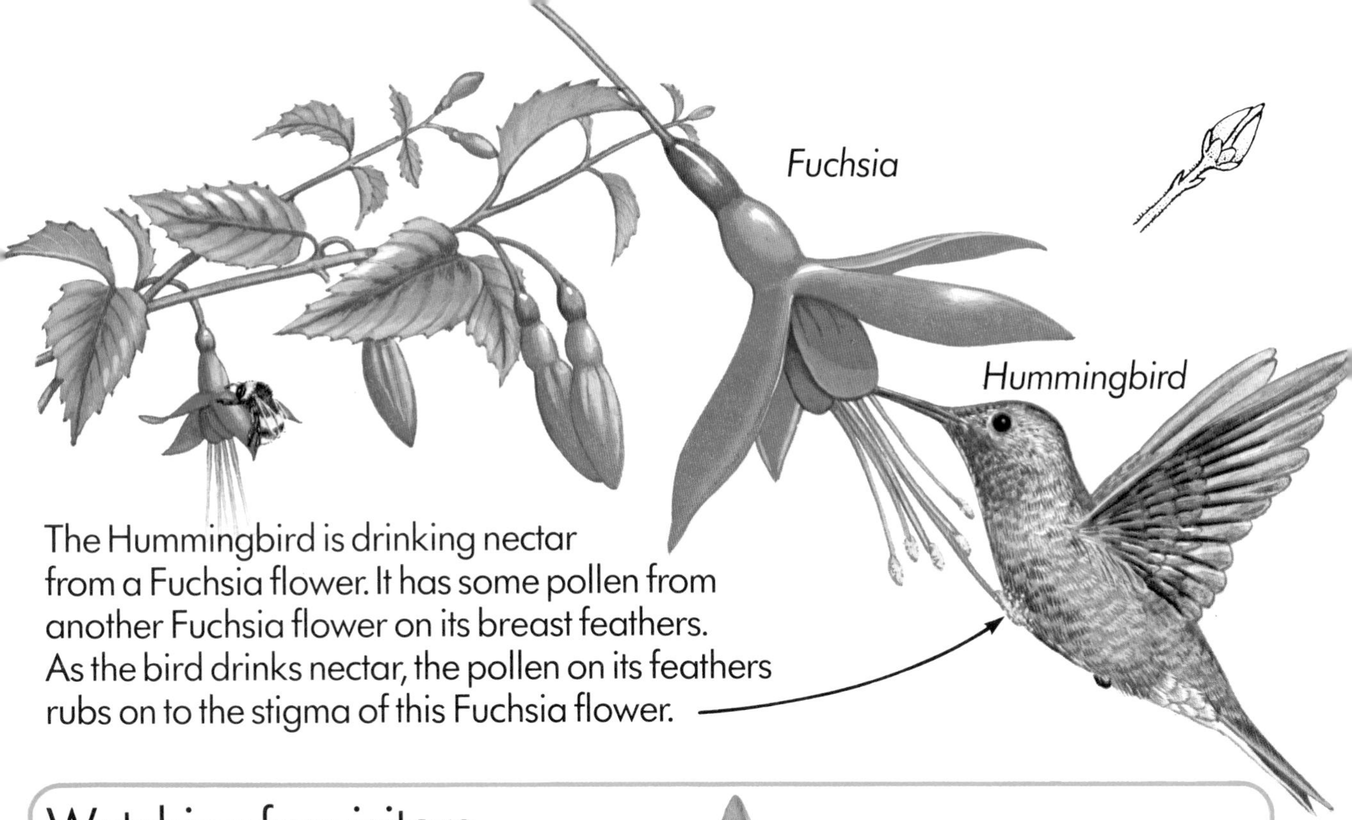

The Hummingbird is drinking nectar from a Fuchsia flower. It has some pollen from another Fuchsia flower on its breast feathers. As the bird drinks nectar, the pollen on its feathers rubs on to the stigma of this Fuchsia flower.

Watching for visitors

Find a flower that has stamens and a stigma that are easy to see. When the sun is out, sit down and wait for the insects to come.

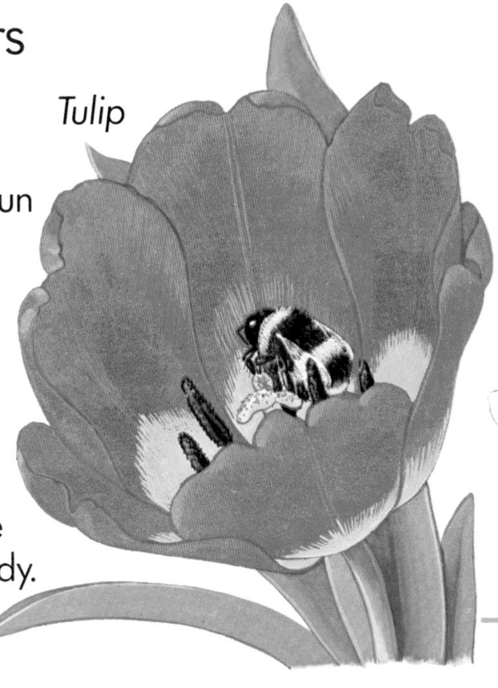

If an insect comes, try to see if it has any pollen on its body.

When the insect flies away, look to see if it has left any pollen on the stigma of your flower.

How the wind helps flowers

The flowers on this page do not need visitors to move their pollen. The wind blows their pollen from flower to flower.

Plantain flowers

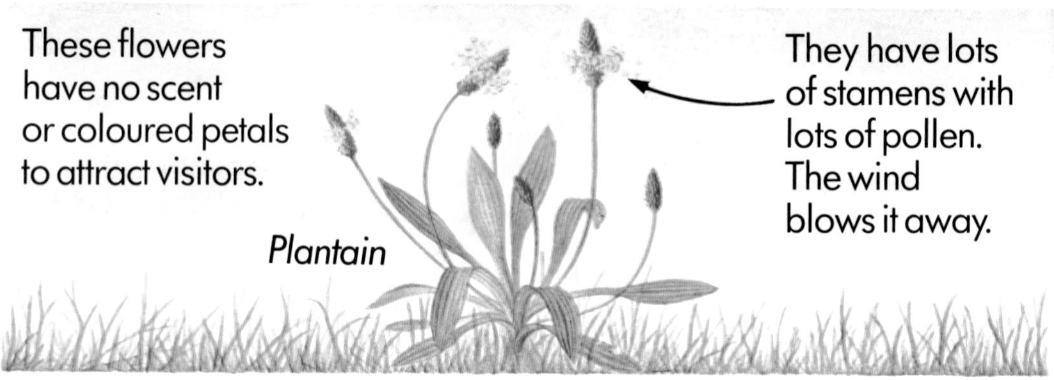
These flowers have no scent or coloured petals to attract visitors.
Plantain
They have lots of stamens with lots of pollen. The wind blows it away.

False Oat Grass flowers

In spring you may see clouds of pollen blowing off grass flowers. Most of this pollen will be wasted, but some will stick on to the stigmas of the grass flowers.

Wood-Rush flowers

Rye flowers

All trees have flowers. Many trees use the wind to move their pollen.

The Walnut Tree has two kinds of flowers. One kind of flower has a large pistil. The other kind of flower is made of lots of stamens.

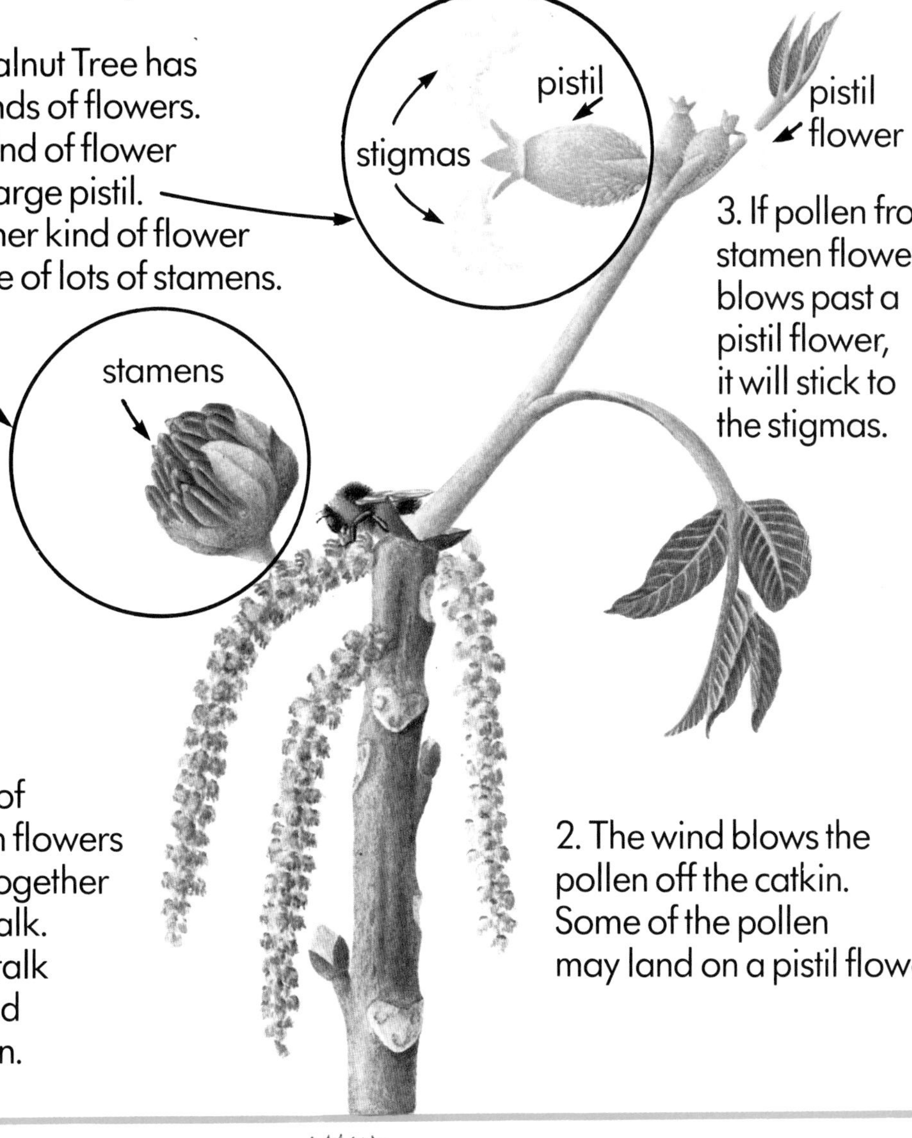

1. Lots of stamen flowers grow together on a stalk. Each stalk is called a catkin.

2. The wind blows the pollen off the catkin. Some of the pollen may land on a pistil flower.

3. If pollen from stamen flowers blows past a pistil flower, it will stick to the stigmas.

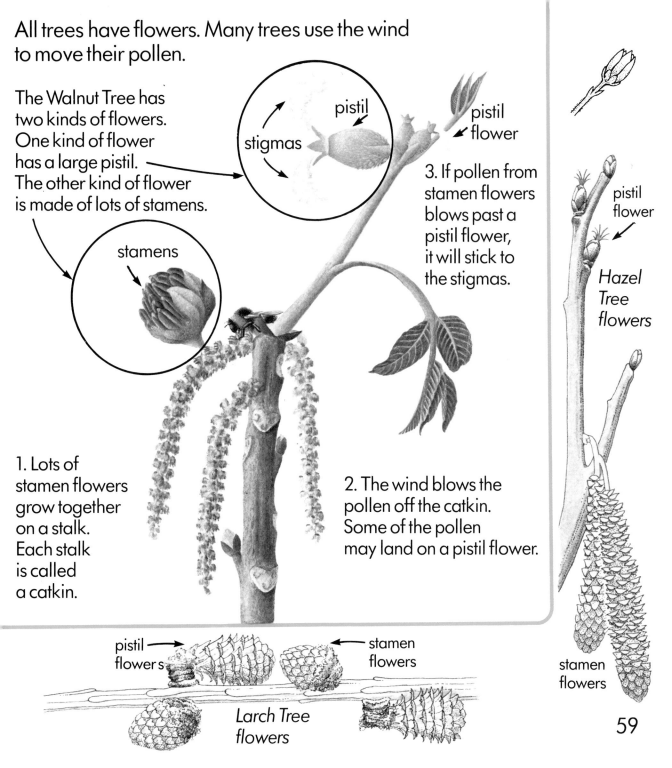

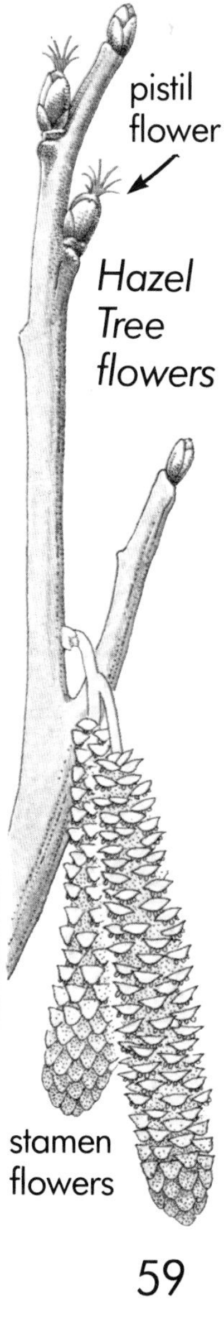

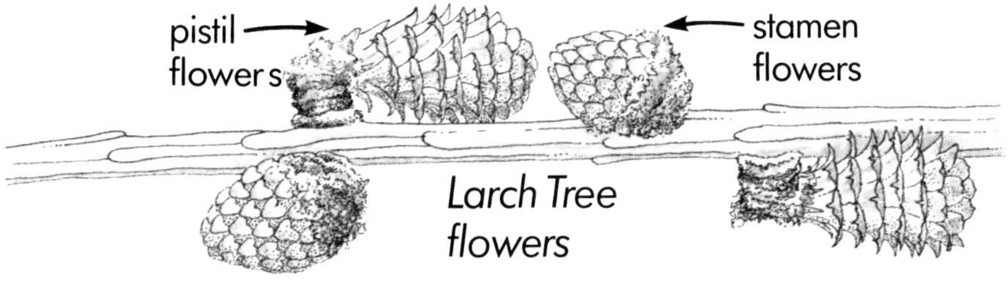

What happens to the pollen

1. A bee has left pollen on this stigma. The pollen came from another Poppy flower.

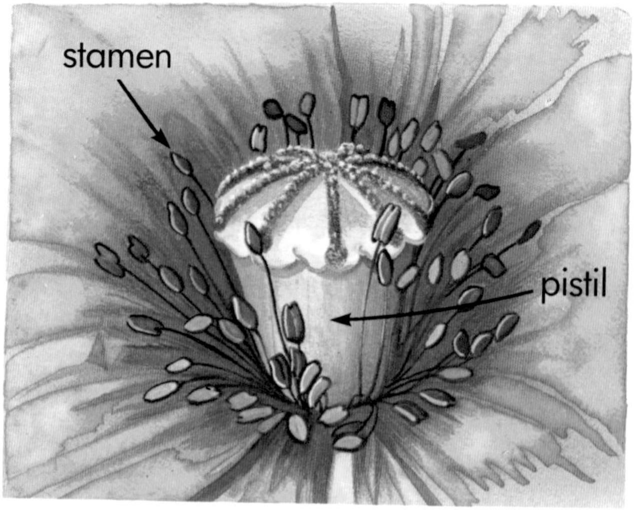

2. Each grain of pollen grows a tube down inside the pistil.
There are ovules inside the pistil.

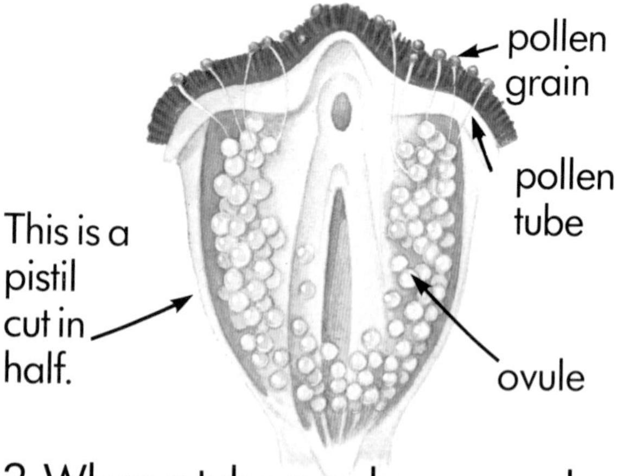

3. When a tube reaches an ovule, the inside of the pollen grain moves out of the tube and joins with the ovule.

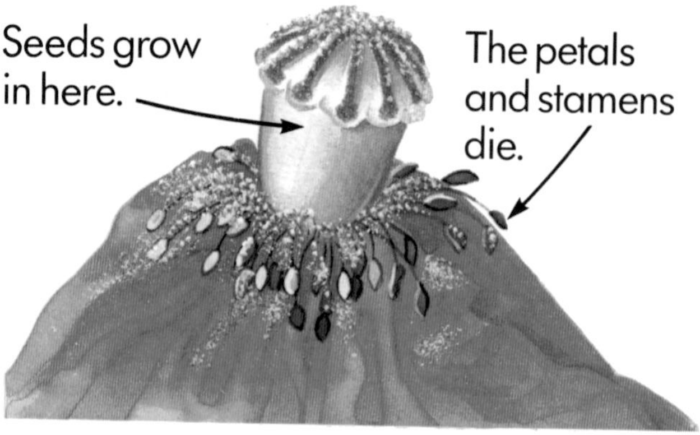

4. The ovules in the pistil have been fertilized by the pollen.
The fertilized ovules will grow into Poppy seeds.

The flowers on the Poppy plant can be fertilized only when an insect brings pollen from another Poppy plant.

A Poppy flower cannot use its own pollen to fertilize its own ovules. The pollen will not grow tubes down into the pistil.

Poppy pollen will not grow tubes in the Buttercup pistil.

More about pollen

Many flowers are like the Poppy. They do not use their own pollen to fertilize themselves. Pollen must be brought from another flower of the same kind by visitors or by the wind.

A single flower of the Yellow Mountain Saxifrage can never fertilize itself because the stamens die before the stigmas are ripe.

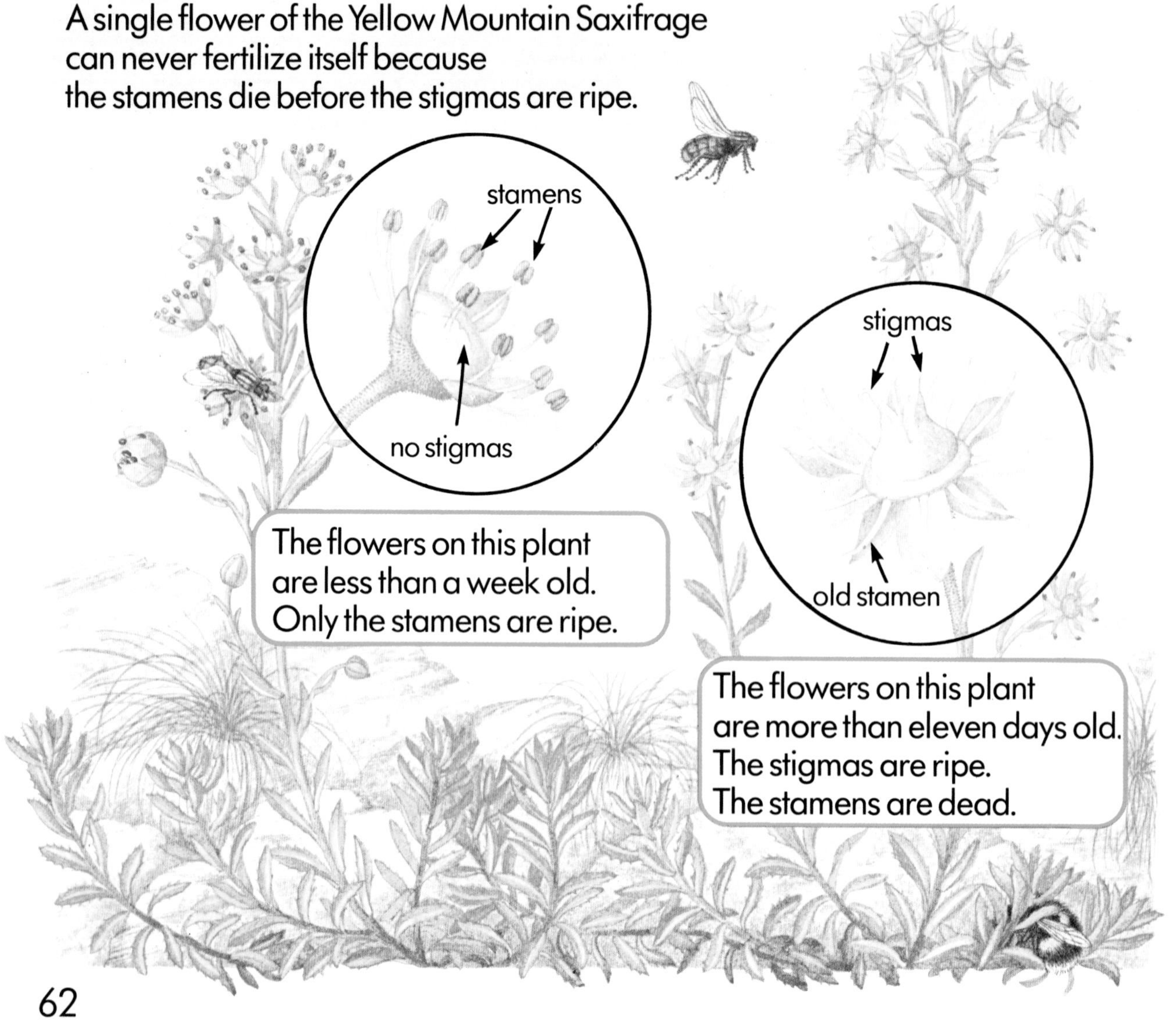

stamens
no stigmas
The flowers on this plant are less than a week old. Only the stamens are ripe.
stigmas
old stamen
The flowers on this plant are more than eleven days old. The stigmas are ripe. The stamens are dead.

The pollen of this Bee Orchid is moved only by male Eucera Bees. But if no Eucera Bees visit the Orchid it will use its own pollen to fertilize itself.

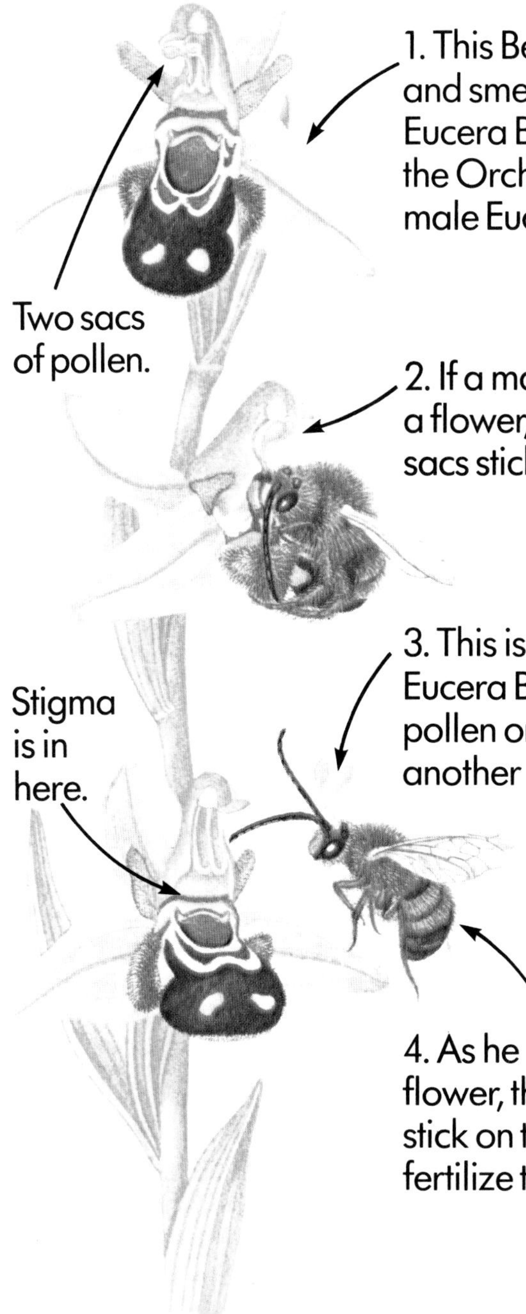

1. This Bee Orchid looks and smells like a female Eucera Bee. This is how the Orchid attracts male Eucera Bees.

2. If a male Bee lands on a flower, the two pollen sacs stick on to his head.

3. This is another male Eucera Bee. He has pollen on his head from another Bee Orchid.

4. As he lands on this flower, the pollen will stick on to the stigma and fertilize the flower.

If no Bees visit this Bee Orchid, it will fertilize itself.

This is how the Bee Orchid fertilizes itself.

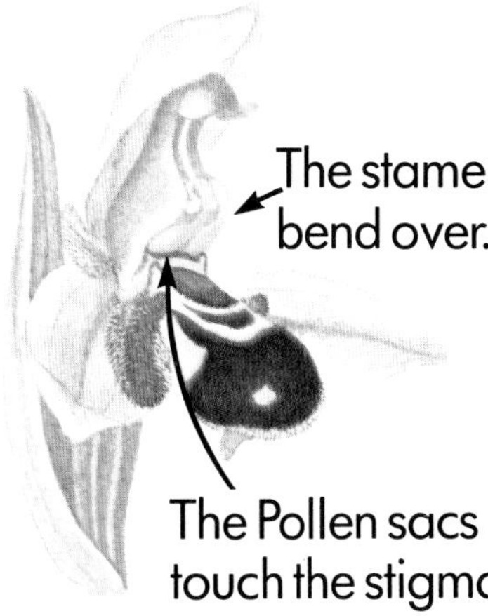

The stamens bend over.
The Pollen sacs touch the stigma.

How seeds leave the plant

1. The ovules in this Poppy pistil have been fertilized. They are growing into seeds.

2. The pistil swells. It is now a fruit with seeds inside it.

3. Holes open in the top. When the wind blows the fruit, the seeds fall out.

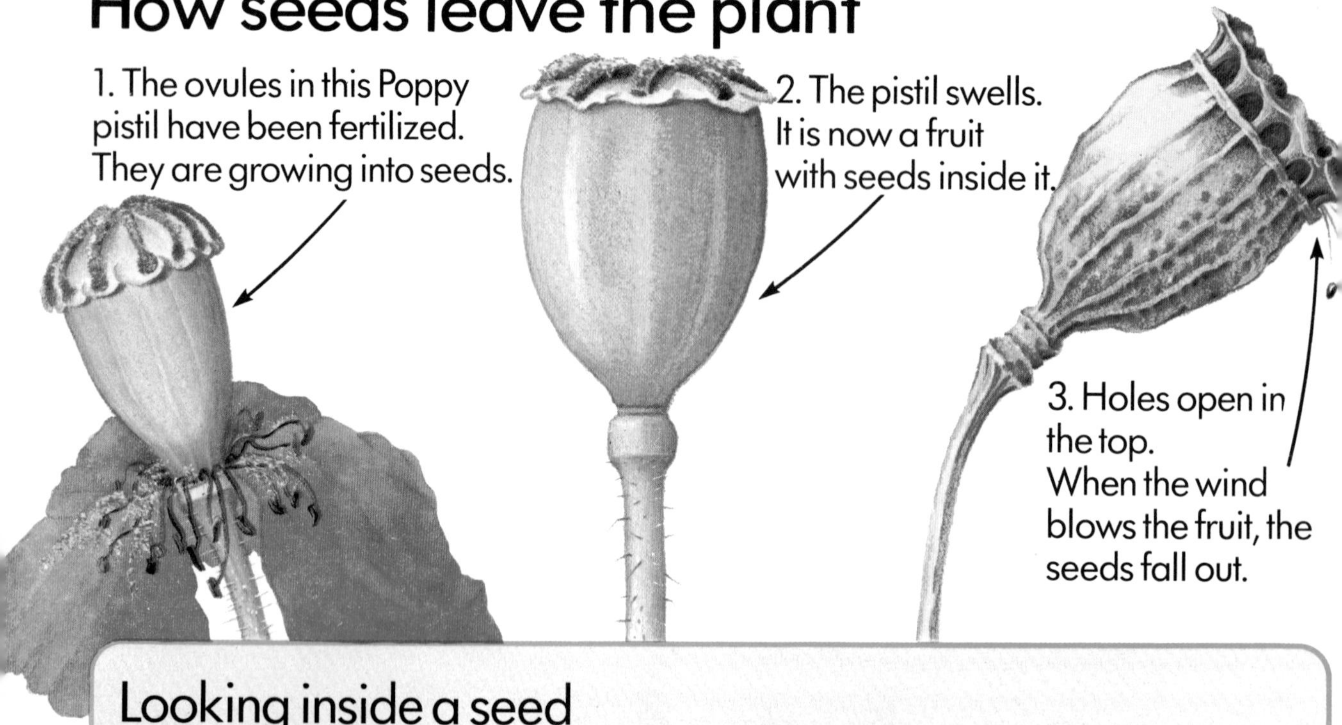

Looking inside a seed

This is a bean seed. It has a thick skin to protect the parts inside.

If you split open a bean seed, this is what you will see inside.

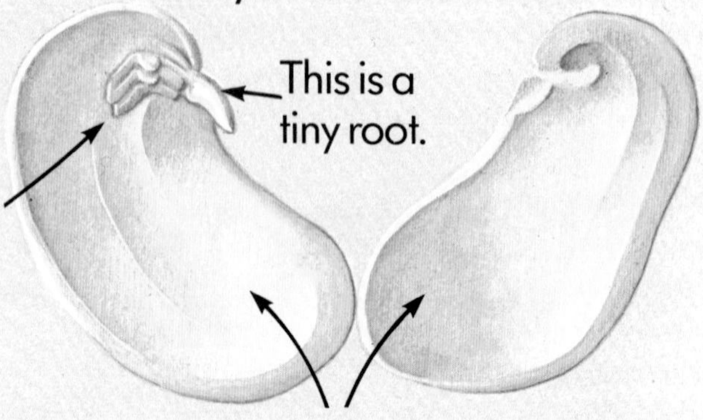

This is a tiny root.

This tiny shoot will grow into a new plant.

These are two seed leaves full of food. The shoot will use this food when it grows.

When the seeds in the fruits are ripe, the wind or animals may move them away from the plant.

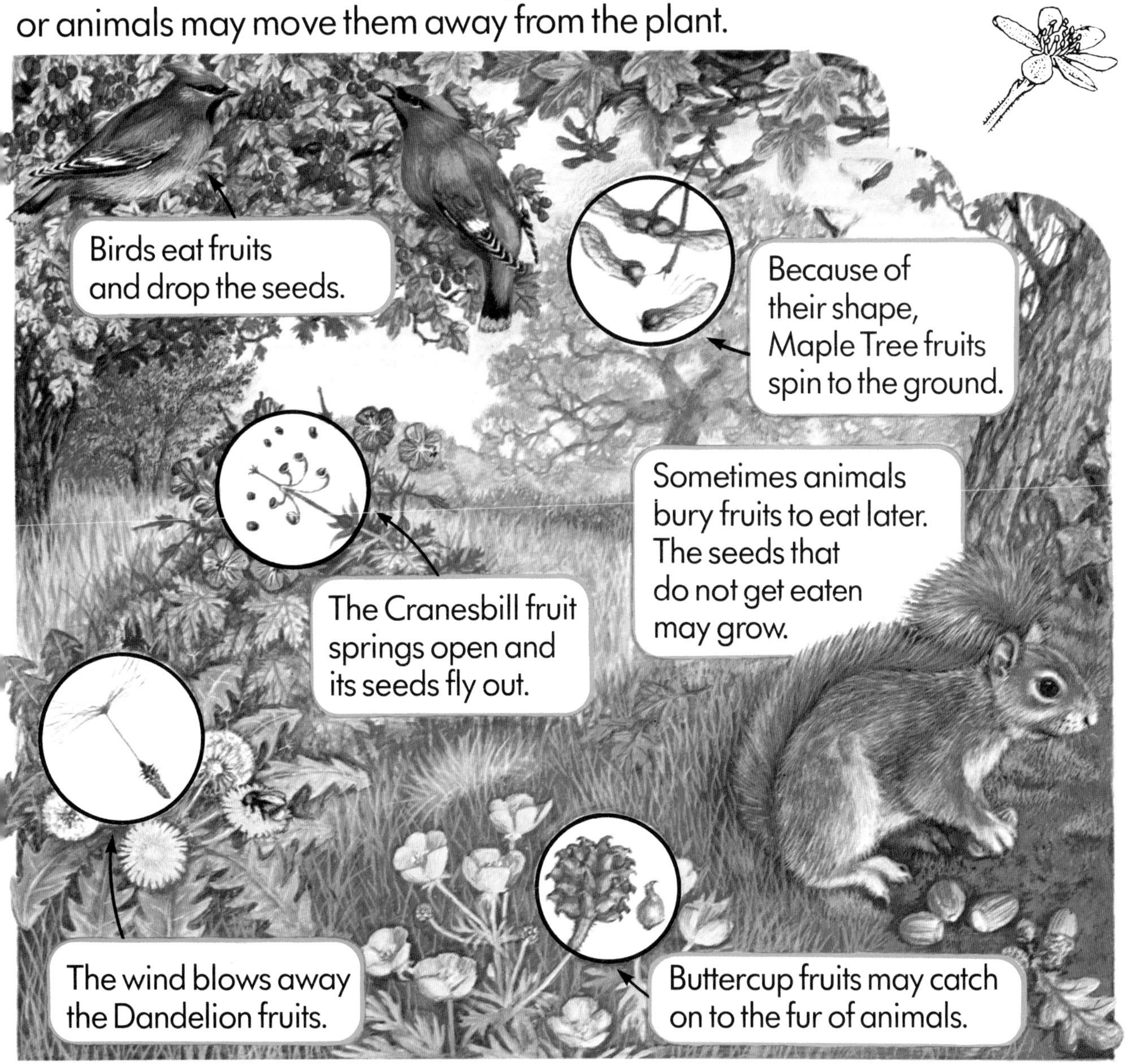

Birds eat fruits and drop the seeds.
Because of their shape, Maple Tree fruits spin to the ground.
Sometimes animals bury fruits to eat later. The seeds that do not get eaten may grow.
The Cranesbill fruit springs open and its seeds fly out.
The wind blows away the Dandelion fruits.
Buttercup fruits may catch on to the fur of animals.

Plants make lots of seeds but only a few of the seeds will grow into new plants. The others die or get eaten.

How a seed grows

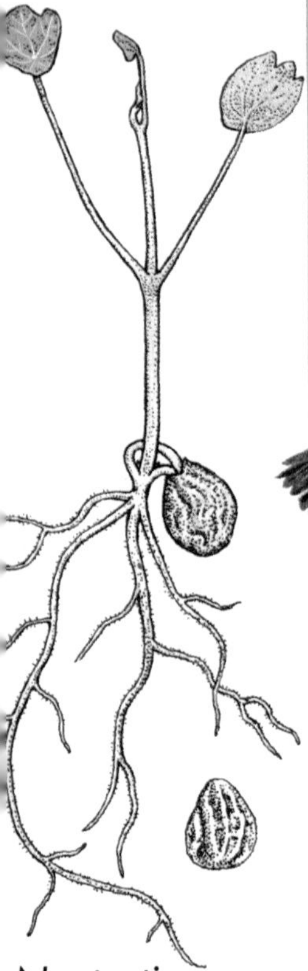

Nasturtium

1. Autumn

A bird drops
a Sunflower seed
by accident.

2. Winter

The seed falls to the
ground and gets
covered over.

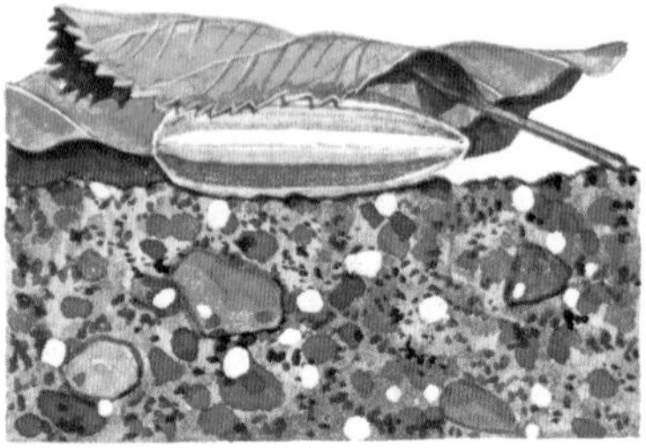

3. Spring

Rain makes the
seed swell.
A root grows down
into the soil.

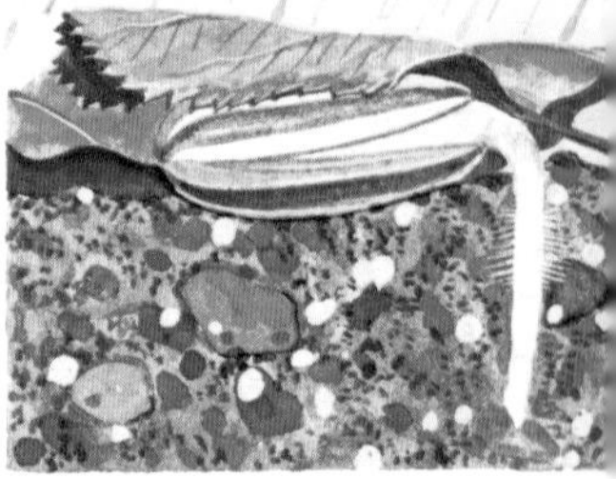

6. Late spring

The Sunflower plant
grows a flower bud.
The plant is now
taller than a person.

7. Summer

The
buds
open.

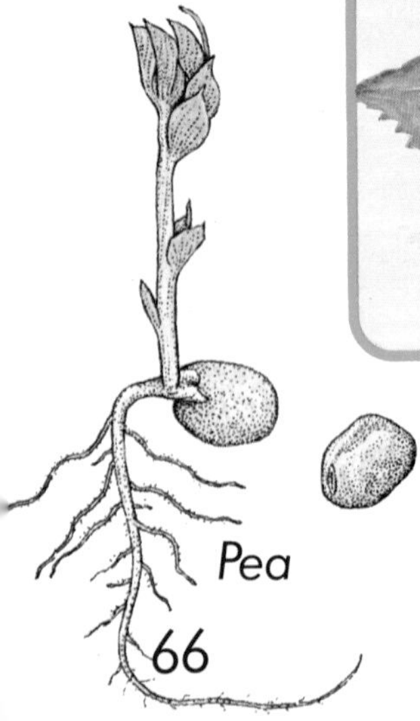

Pea

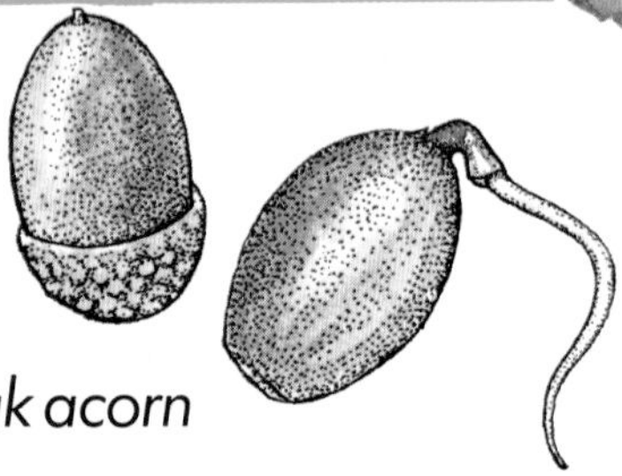

Oak acorn

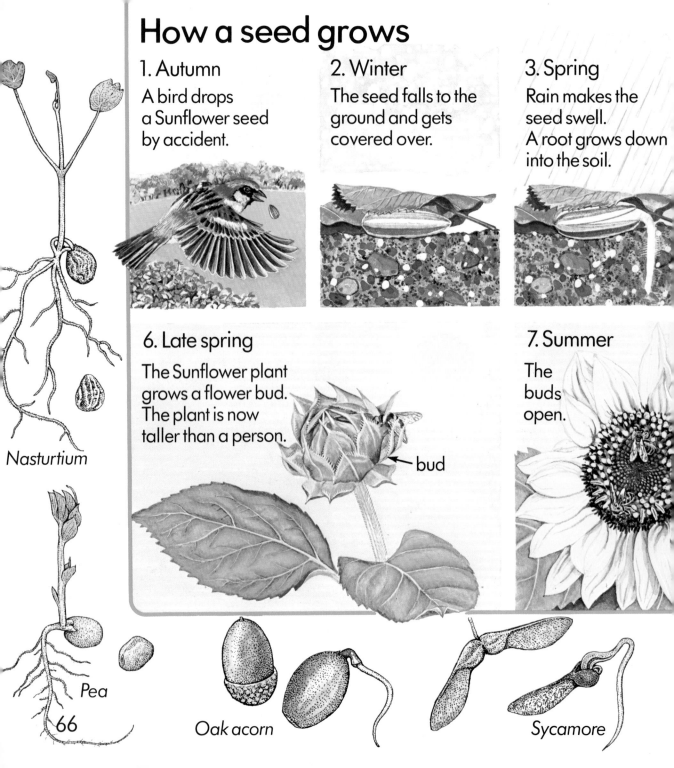

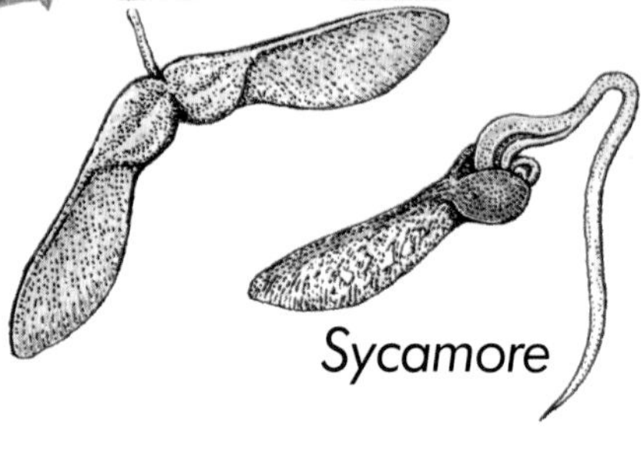

Sycamore

4. Spring

The shoot grows towards the light.

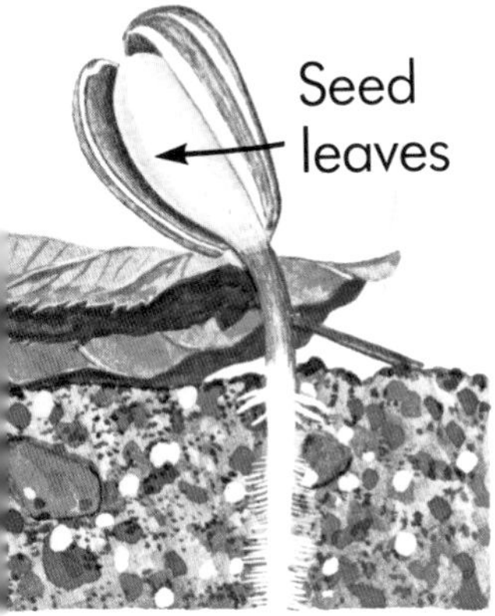

Seed
leaves

5. Spring

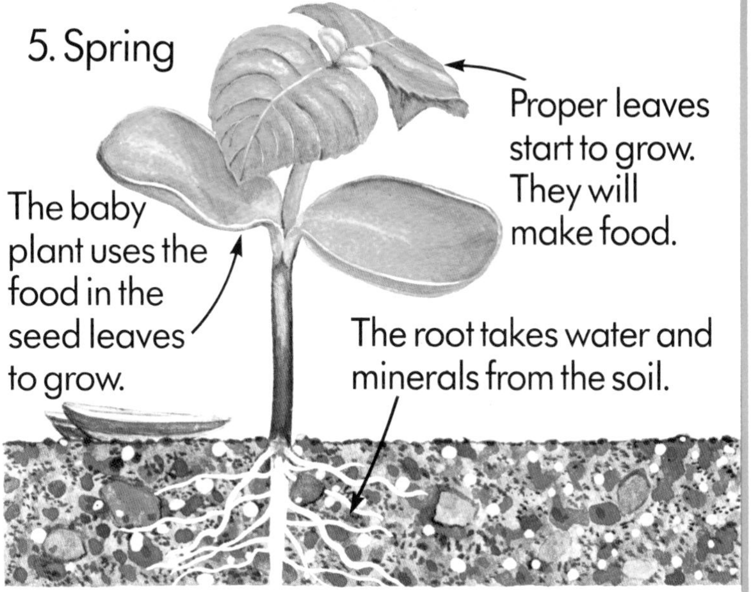

The baby plant uses the food in the seed leaves to grow.
Proper leaves start to grow. They will make food.
The root takes water and minerals from the soil.

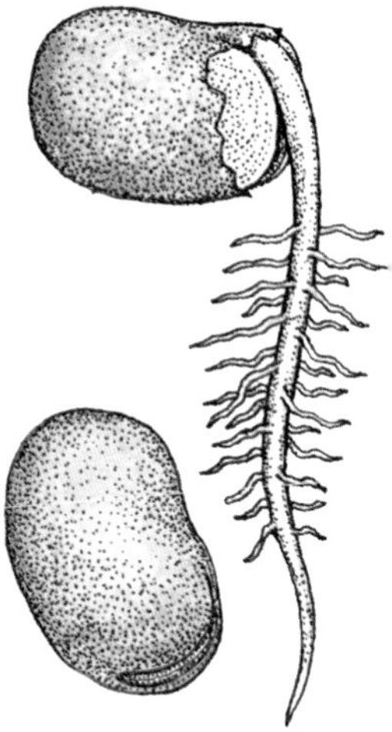

Broad Bean

Bees bring pollen from other Sunflowers.

8. Autumn

The flowers have been fertilized.
A bird eats the seeds.

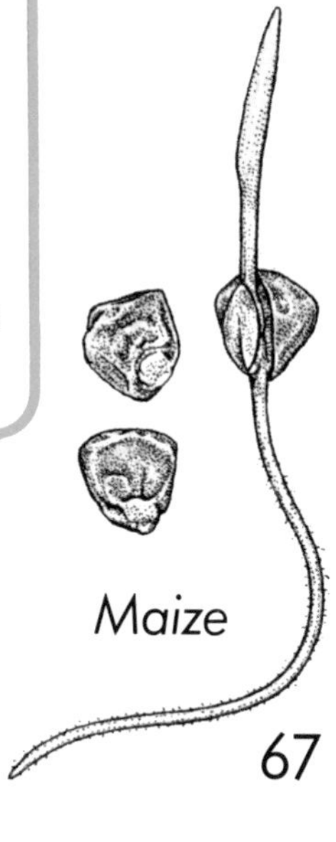

Maize

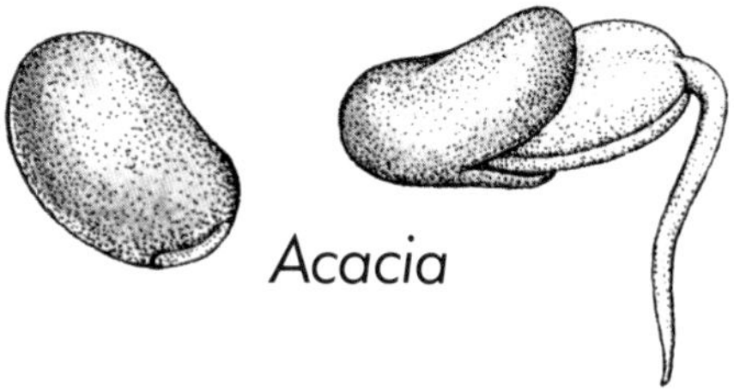

Acacia

Sweet Pea

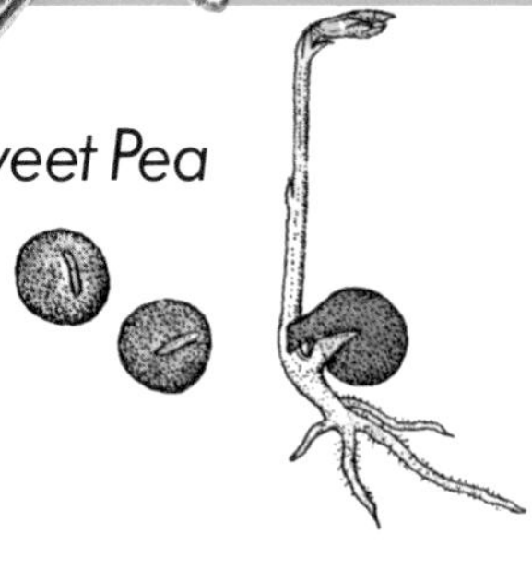

How flowers and insects work together

Flowers make most nectar and scent when their pistil or stamens are ripe because this is when they need to attract visitors.

Bees visit these Cherry flowers in the morning. This is when the flowers have most nectar.

Bees visit these Apple flowers in the afternoon. This is when the flowers have most nectar.

New Honeysuckle flowers open in the evening. This is when moths visit them.

The flowers make lots of scent in the evening, but only a little scent in the day.

Many plants take several weeks to open all their flowers. Bees come back to these plants day after day until all the flowers are over.

The Willowherb takes about a month to open all its flowers. The first flowers to open are at the bottom of the stem. The last flowers to open are at the top of the stem.

Willowherb or *Fireweed*

Horse Chestnut Tree flowers

New flowers open every day. They have lots of nectar. Yellow guide-lines point the way to the nectar.

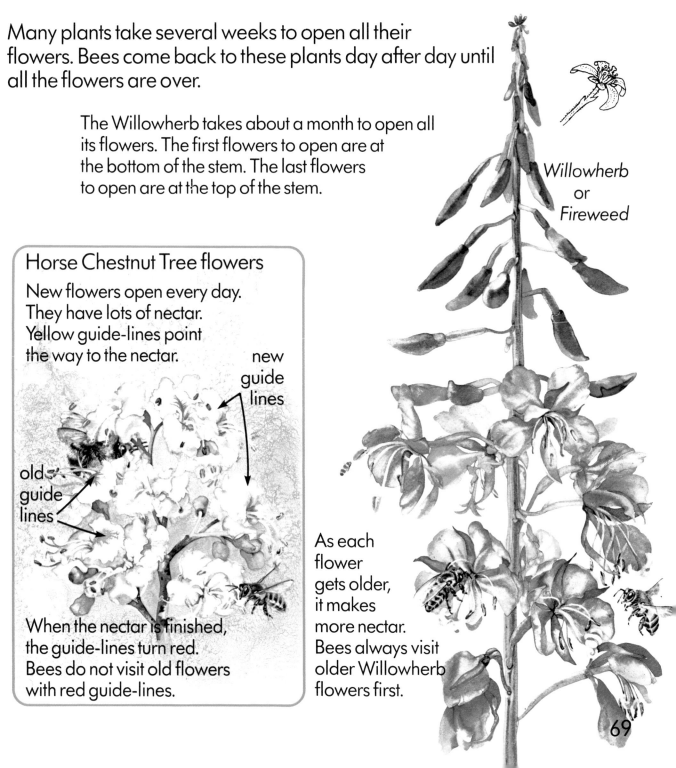

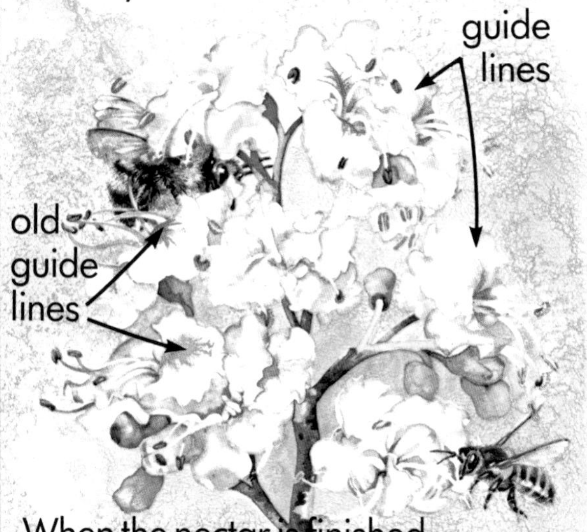

When the nectar is finished, the guide-lines turn red. Bees do not visit old flowers with red guide-lines.

As each flower gets older, it makes more nectar. Bees always visit older Willowherb flowers first.

Keeping pollen safe

Most flowers try to keep their pollen safe and dry. Cold weather, rain and dew could damage the pollen or wash it away.

When flowers are closed, the pollen is kept safe.

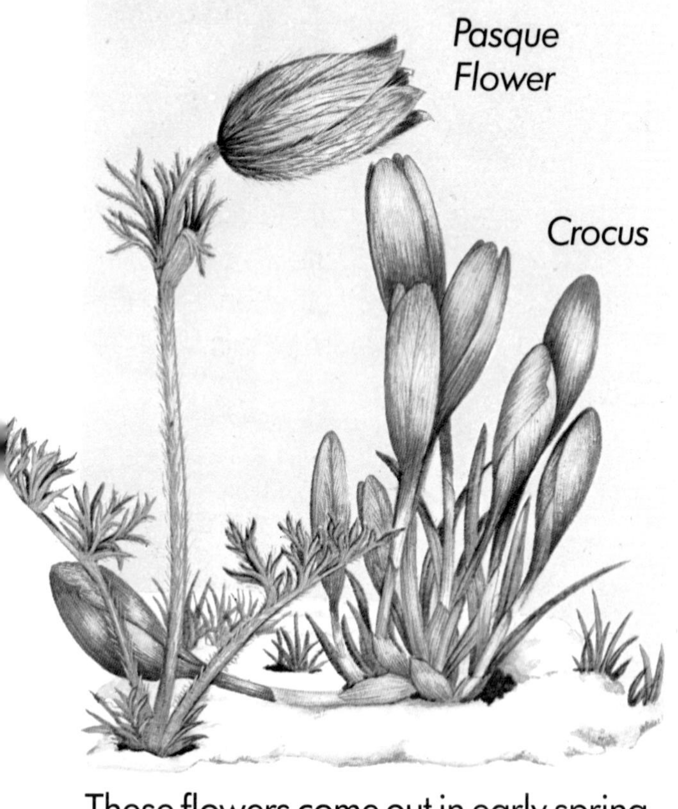

These flowers come out in early spring. The flowers open only when it is warm and sunny. If the sun goes in, they close up their petals. The flowers open again when the sun comes out.

When flowers are closed, rain and dew cannot get inside.

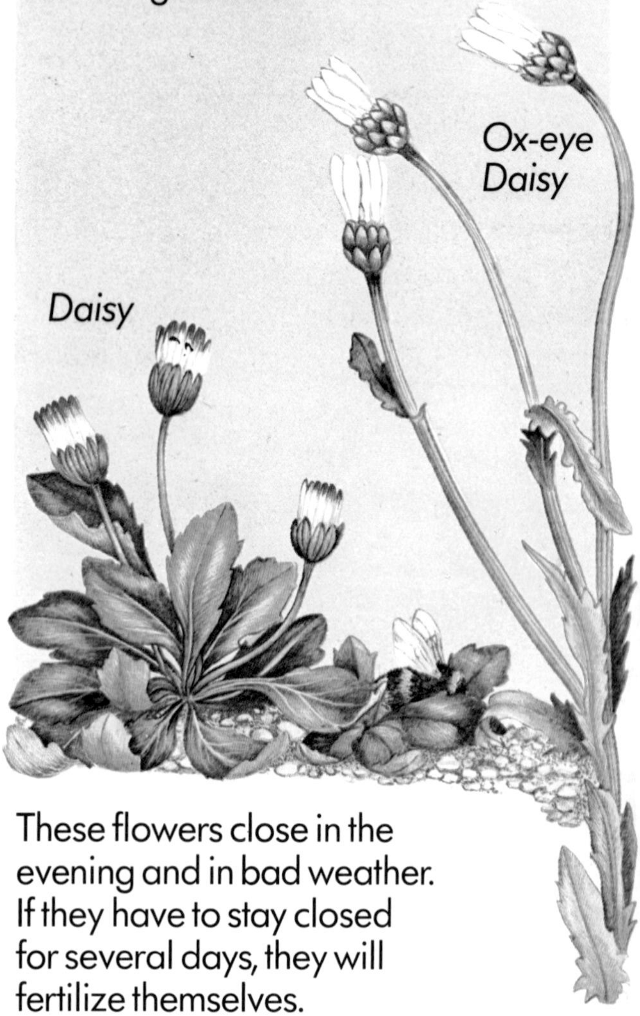

These flowers close in the evening and in bad weather. If they have to stay closed for several days, they will fertilize themselves.

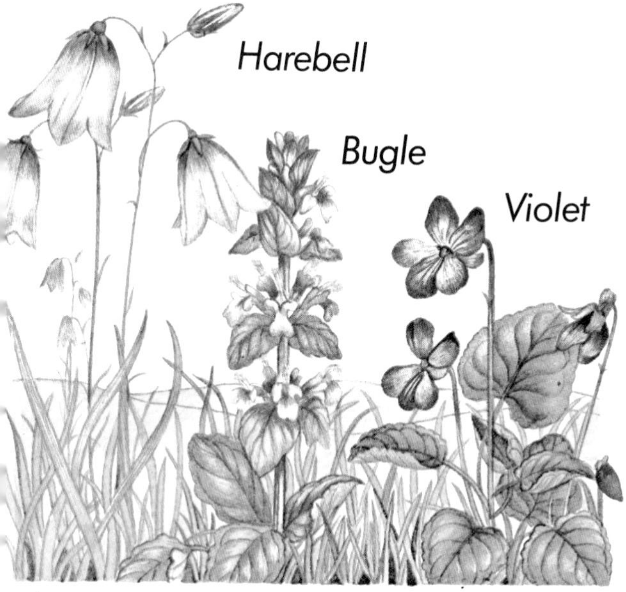

These flowers do not need to close their petals to keep pollen safe. Water cannot collect inside them.

The stamens and the pistil of the Broom flower are kept safe inside the petals. They spring out when a bee lands on the bottom petals.

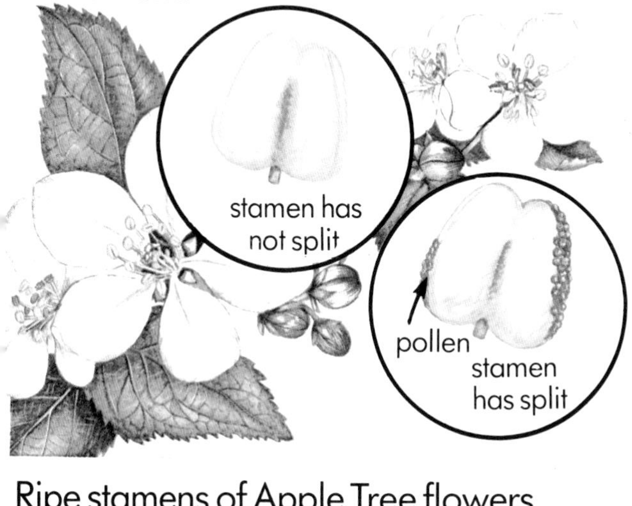

Ripe stamens of Apple Tree flowers split open to let out the pollen. The stamens will split open only on warm days.

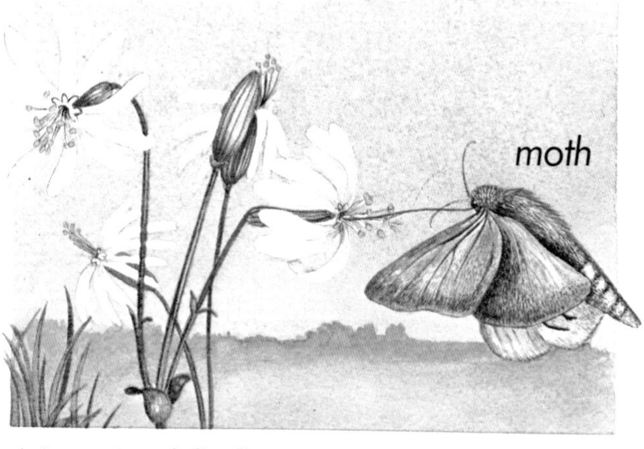

New Catchfly flowers open in the evening. This is when moths visit them. But if the evenings are very cold, no new flowers will open.

Picture puzzle

There are nine flowers and nine fruits on this page. Can you guess which fruits belong to which flowers? You can see most of them in this book.

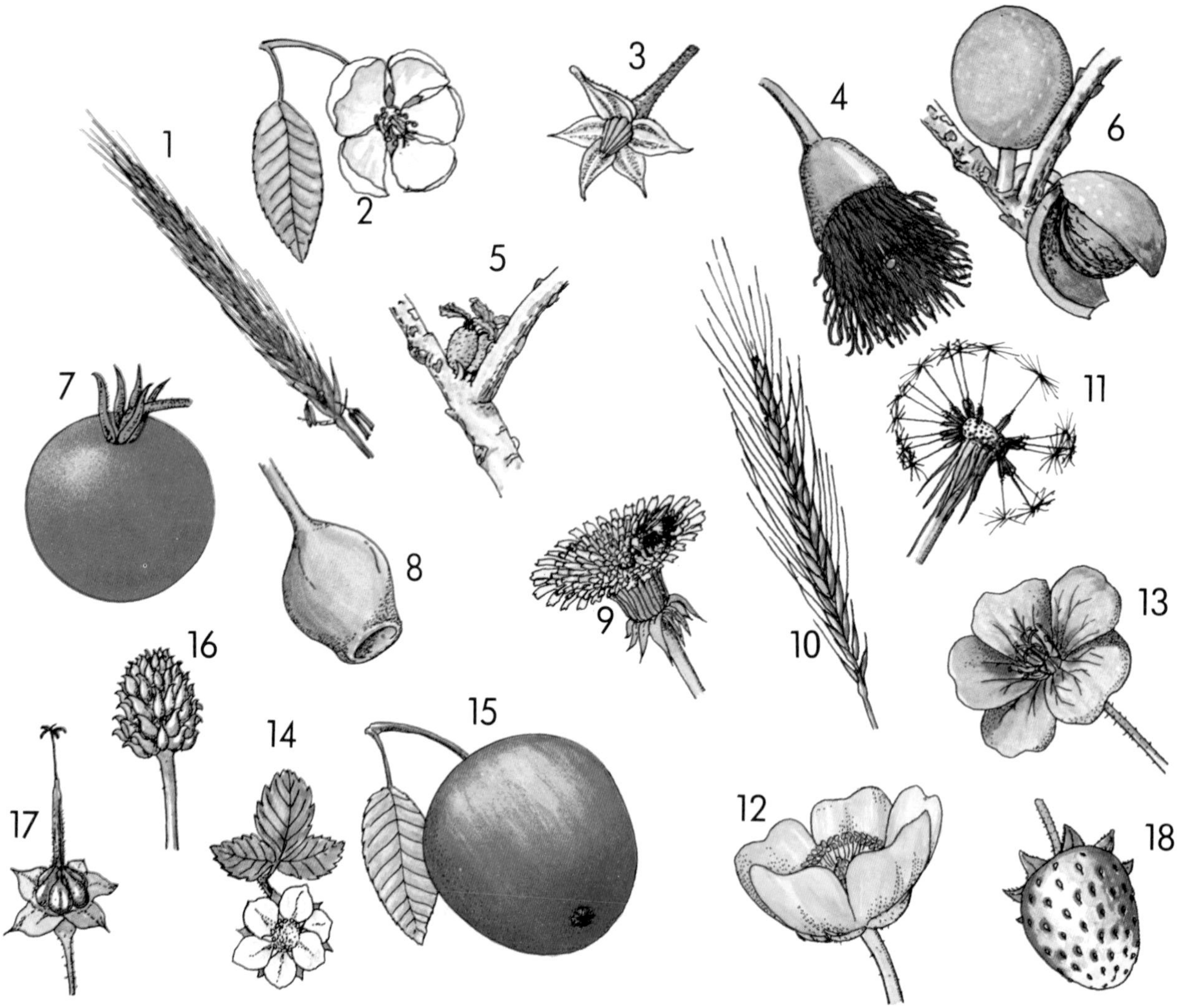

Answers: 1 and 10 Rye. 2 and 15 Apple. 3 and 7 Tomato. 4 and 8 Red Flowering Gum Tree. 5 and 6 Walnut. 9 and 11 Dandelion. 12 and 16 Buttercup. 13 and 17 Cranesbill. 14 and 18 Strawberry.

BUTTERFLIES AND MOTHS

Games

1. Hunt the little green caterpillar

Can you find 11 caterpillars like this in the Butterfly pages?

2. Watch the butterfly move

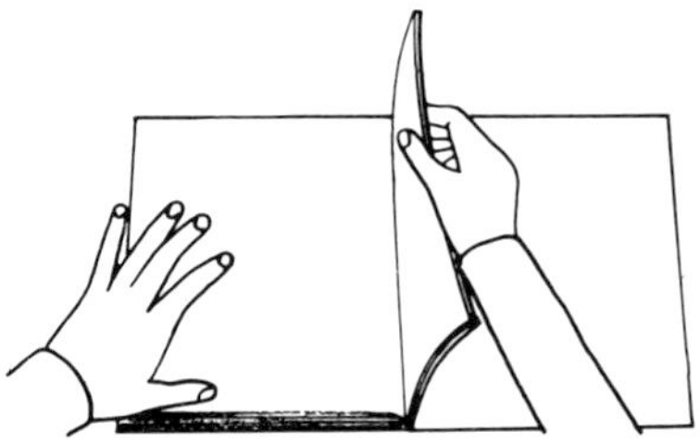

Hold the Butterfly pages like this.

Watch the top right hand corner and flick the pages over fast.

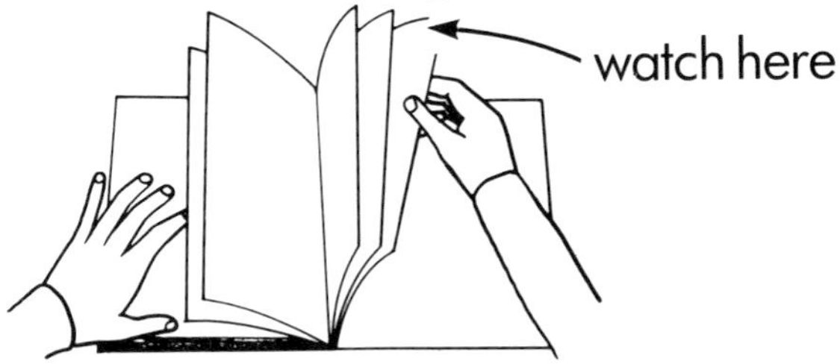

Looking at butterflies and moths

How are all these insects the same?

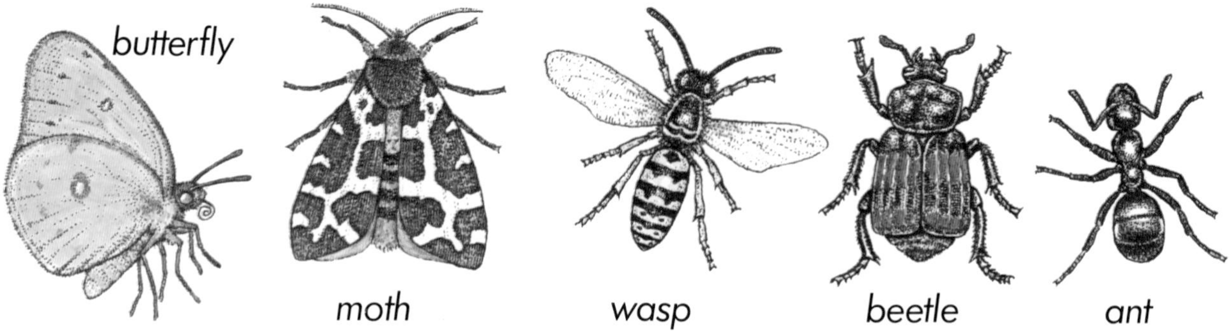

Their bodies are made up of three parts and they all have six legs.

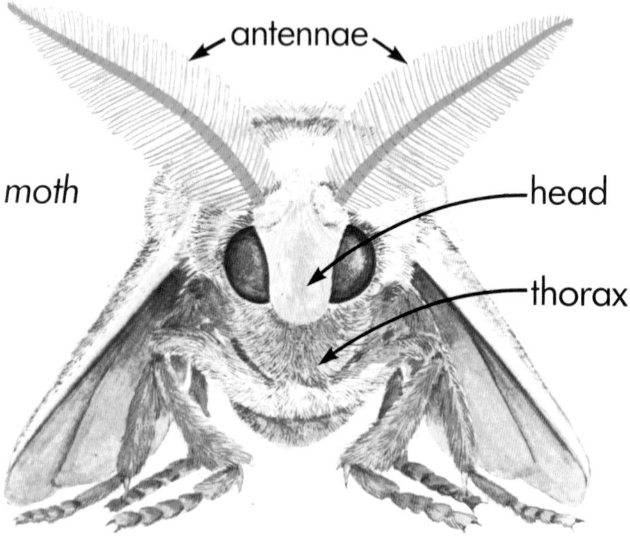

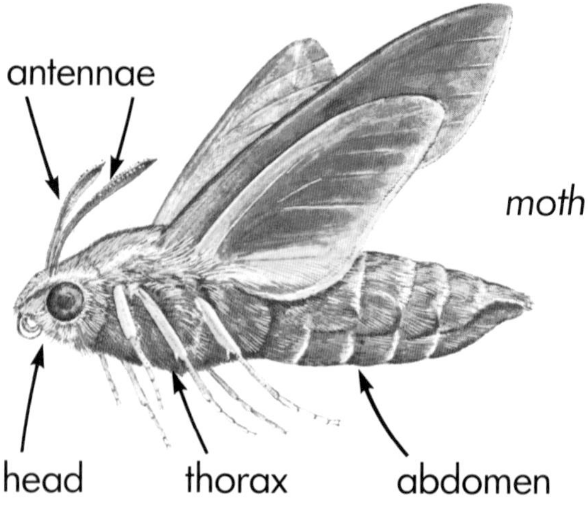

Butterflies and moths have hooks on their feet for holding on tight. They feel and smell with their long antennae.

Behind the head is the thorax. The wings join on to the thorax. The long part of the body is called the abdomen.

Some insects have four wings, some have two wings and some have no wings. How many wings have butterflies and moths got?

The wings are not joined together, but they move together when the butterfly flies.

Swallowtail Butterfly

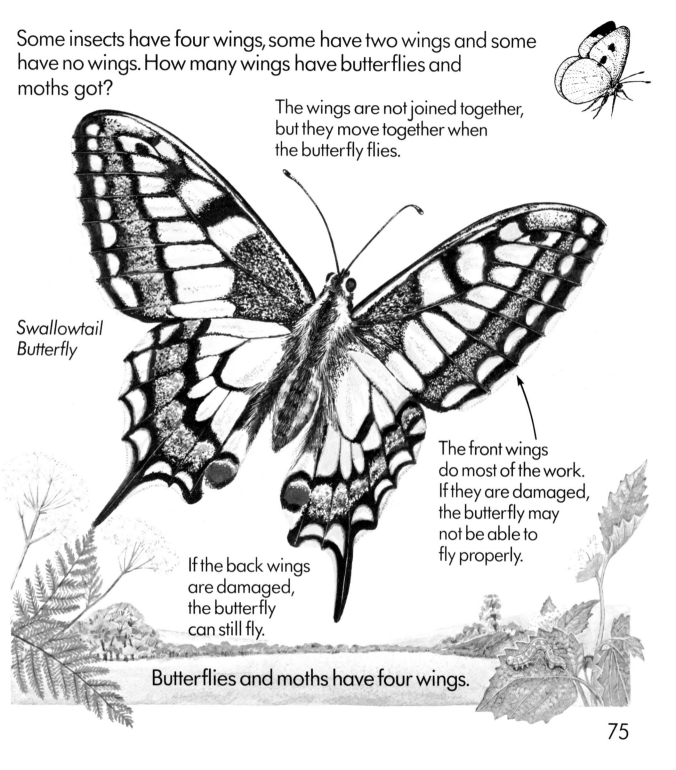

The front wings do most of the work. If they are damaged, the butterfly may not be able to fly properly.

If the back wings are damaged, the butterfly can still fly.

Butterflies and moths have four wings.

Looking at wings

Red Underwing Moth

Oleander Hawk Moth

Walnut Moth

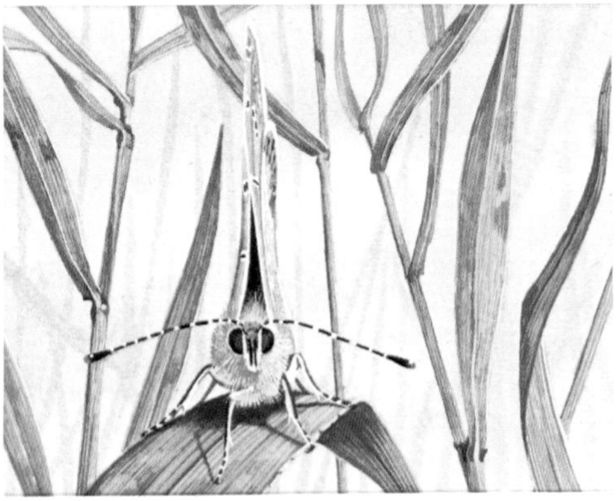

When butterflies rest, they usually close their wings above their backs.

When moths rest, they fold their wings over their backs, or spread them out flat.

Common Blue Butterfly

The wings of a butterfly or moth are often one colour on the outside and a different colour on the inside.

Privet Hawk Moth

When butterflies and moths rest, the colour of the outside of their wings makes it hard for enemies to see them.

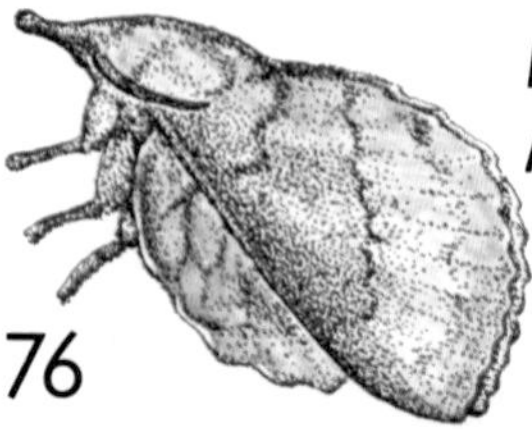

Lappet Moth

Scallop Shell Moth

Small Skipper Butterfly

Some butterflies look like dead leaves when they rest. They are hard to see.

Buff-tip Moth

Some moths look like twigs when they rest. It is hard for enemies to see them.

What makes the colours on their wings?

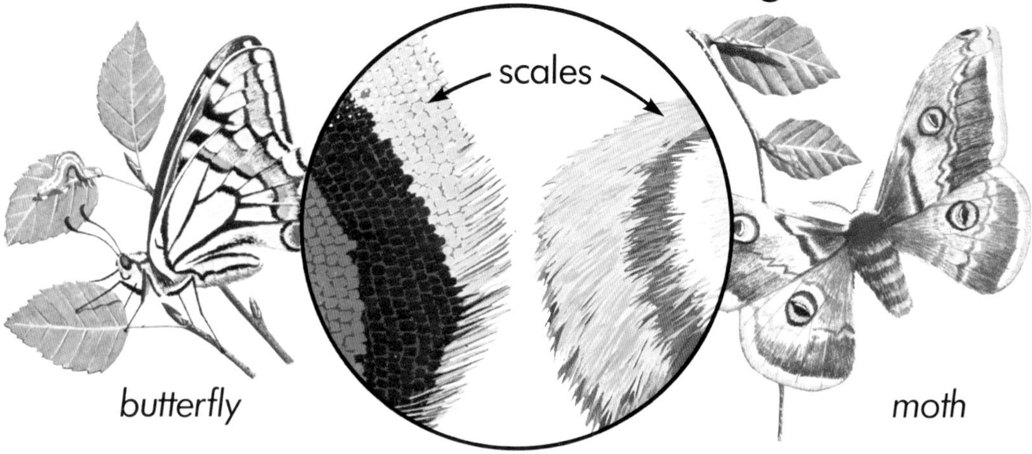

The wings are covered with coloured or shiny scales. If you touch the wings the scales will rub off.

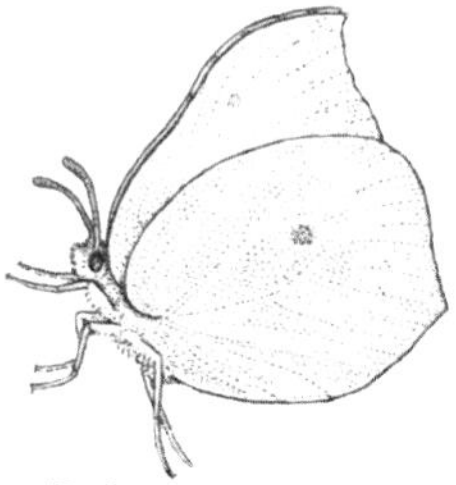

Brimstone Butterfly

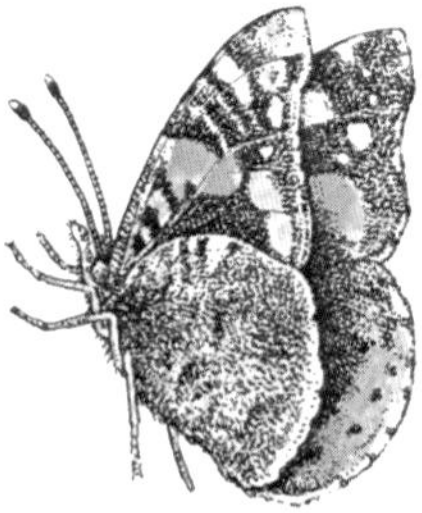

Red Admiral Butterfly

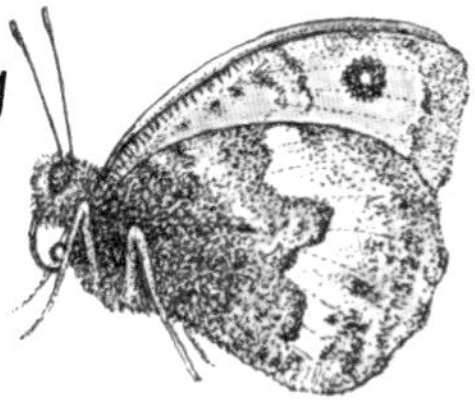

Grayling Butterfly

Green Hairstreak Butterfly

Monarch Butterfly

Keeping warm and feeding

Butterflies and moths need to be warm for their bodies to work properly. When the air is cold, they rest.

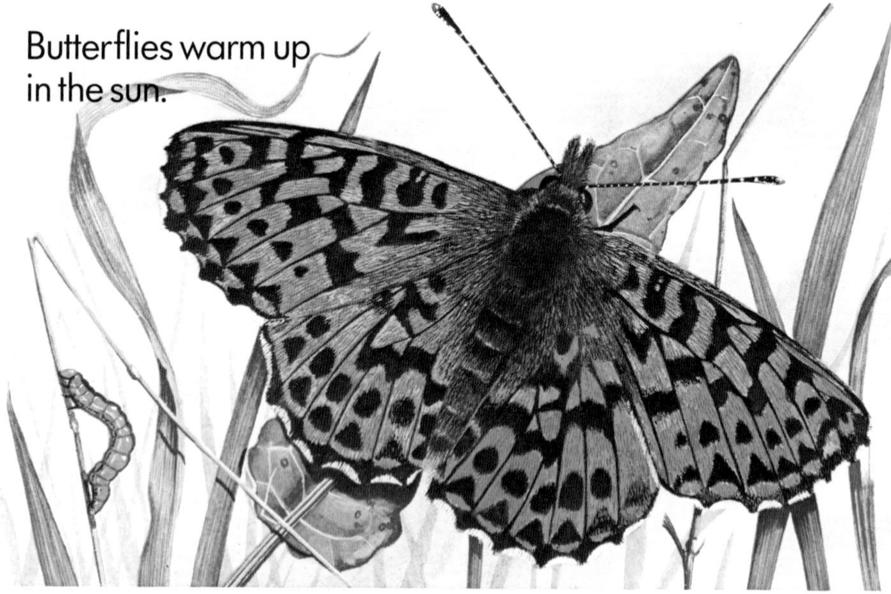

The dark parts of the wings warm up quickly. Butterflies from cold countries often have dark colours on their wings.

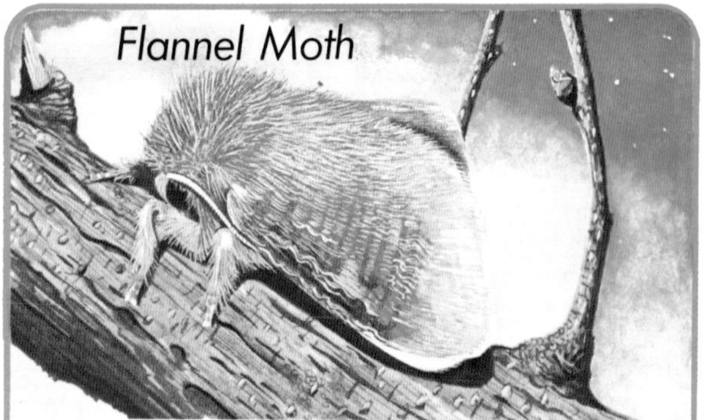

Moths are often very hairy. The hairs on their bodies help to keep them warm at night.

Moths often shiver before they fly. The shivering helps to warm up their bodies.

Butterflies and moths do not eat to grow larger. They use food to make heat inside their bodies. Heat makes energy. This keeps their bodies working.

Moths and butterflies drink a sweet liquid from flowers. This liquid is called nectar.

They drink nectar through a long tube called a proboscis.

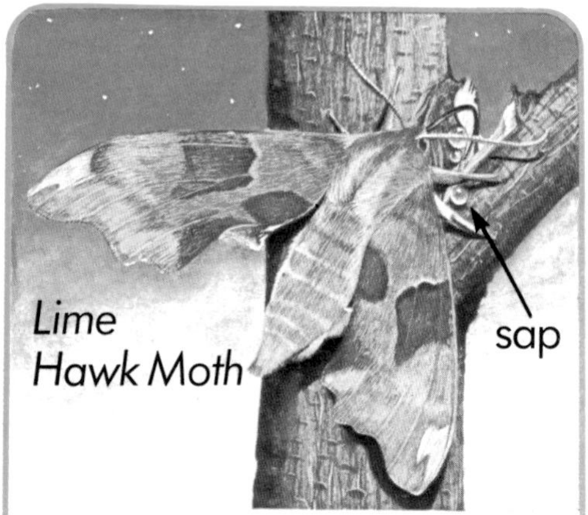

Moths may drink sap from trees or damaged plants.

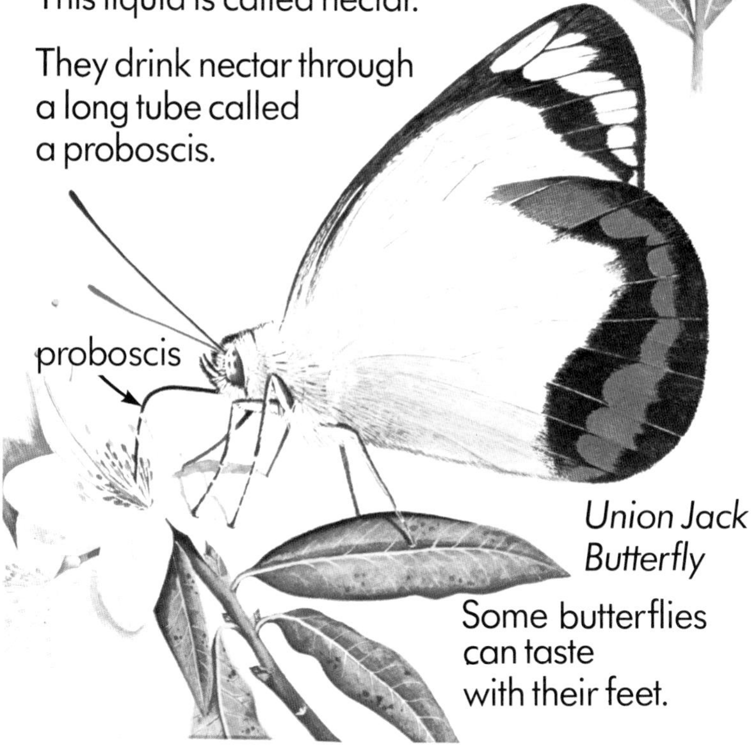

Some butterflies can taste with their feet.

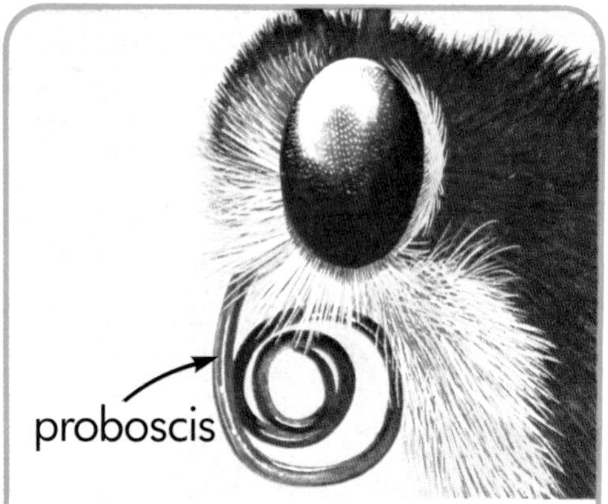

When butterflies and moths are not feeding, their proboscis is curled up.

A butterfly's day

1. The butterfly rests at night when it is cold.

2. When the sun comes out, she warms up.

3. She looks for a place to lay her eggs.

4. She lays her eggs on a special plant.

A moth's night

1. The moth hides in the day.

2. At dusk he shivers to warm himself up.

3. He flies away to find a female.

4. He drinks some nectar from a flower.

5. She warms up again in the sun.

6. Now she is warm enough to fly away.

7. She lands on a flower to drink nectar.

8. When it gets dark and cold, she hides.

5. Now it is very cold so he rests.

6. When it gets warmer, he flies away.

7. He finds a female and mates with her.

8. When it gets light, he hides.

Finding a partner

The most important thing that a butterfly or moth has to do is to find a partner for mating. When a female has mated she will lay her eggs.

male

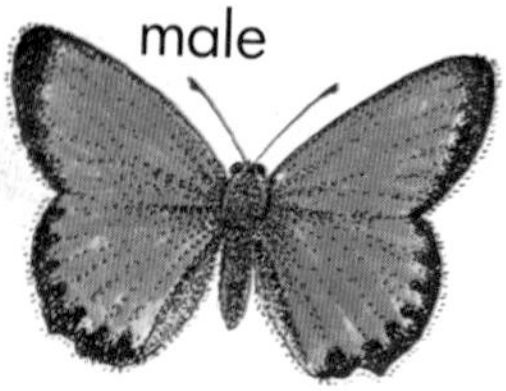

Scarce Copper Butterflies

female

Butterflies use their colours to find each other.

Common Blue Butterflies

female

male

Sometimes the male is a different colour from the female. He may use his colours to show off to her.

male

male

Orange Tip Butterflies

female

The male may have a home area. He will chase out other males and only allow females in.

male

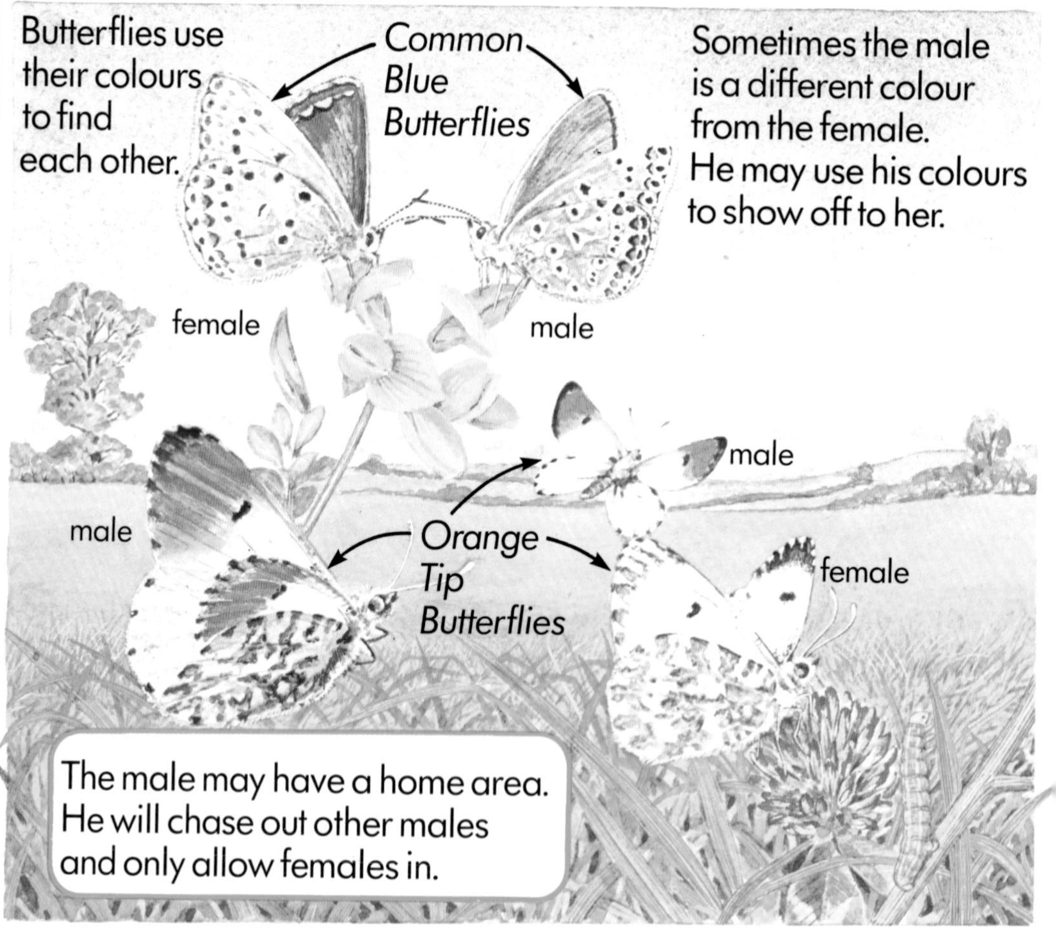

Purple Hairstreak Butterflies

female

female

Swallowtail Butterflies

male

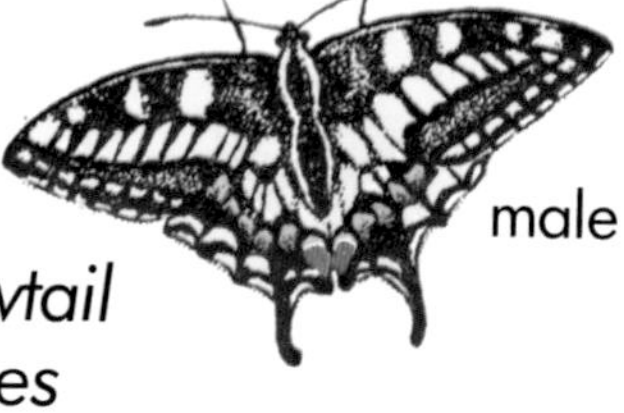

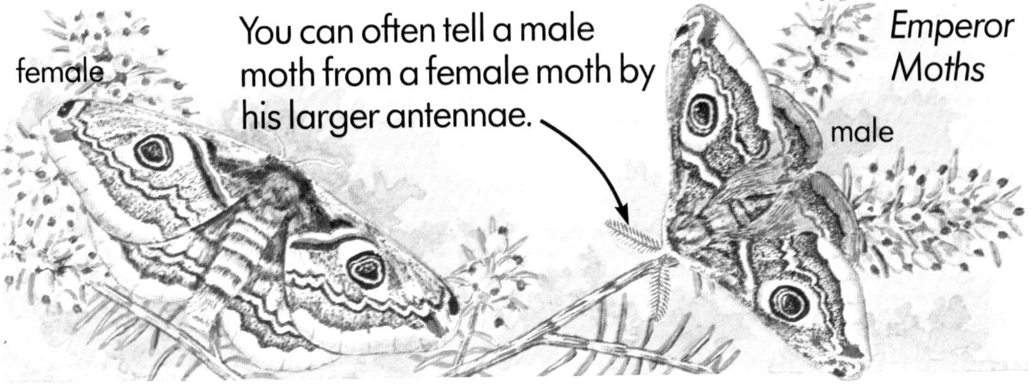

female
You can often tell a male moth from a female moth by his larger antennae.
Emperor Moths
male

At night, moths cannot use colour to find each other. Instead the male finds the female by her scent. Each kind of moth has a different scent.

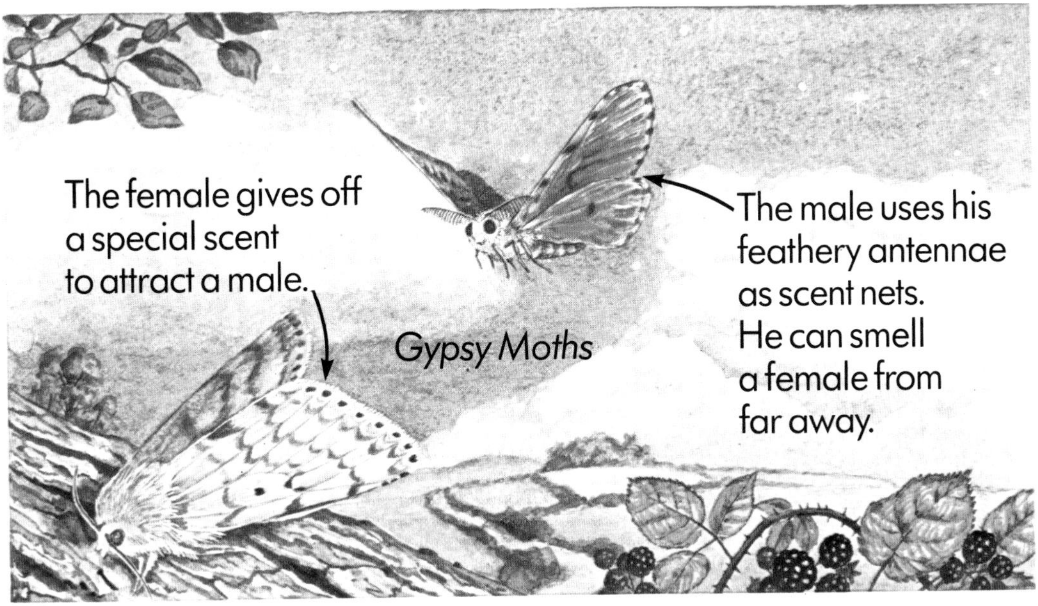

The female gives off a special scent to attract a male.
Gypsy Moths
The male uses his feathery antennae as scent nets. He can smell a female from far away.

male

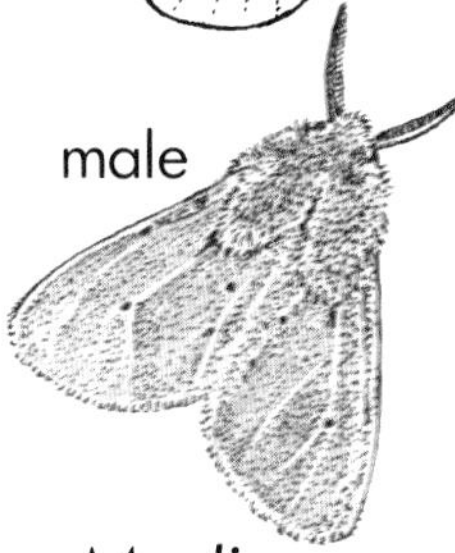

Muslin Moths

female

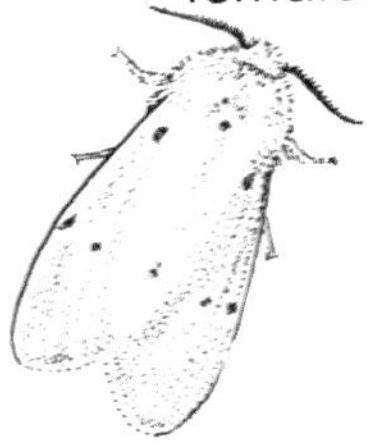

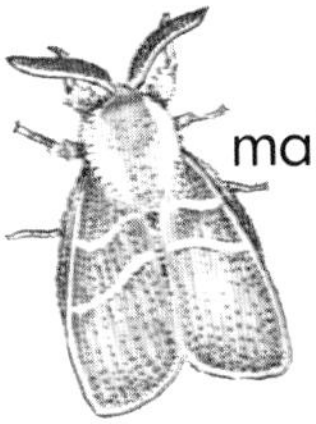

male

Hag Moths

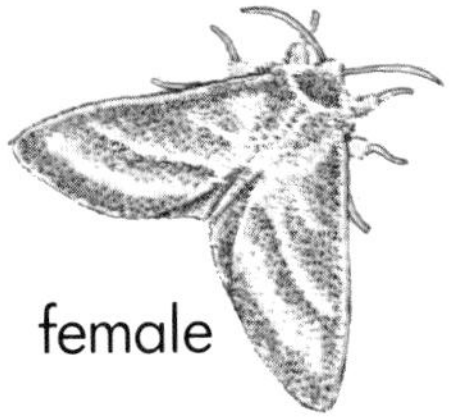

female

female

Oak Eggar Moths

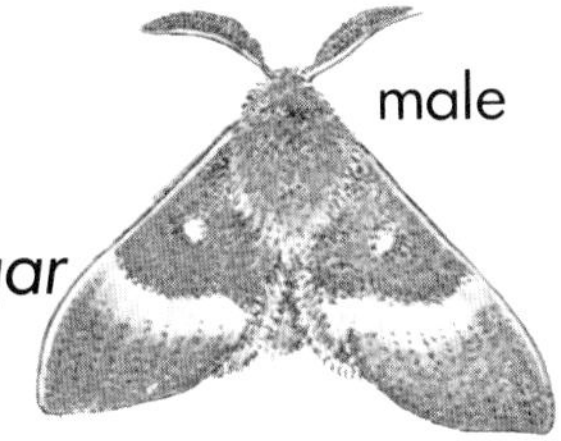

male

Mating and laying eggs

A pair of butterflies may play together before they mate.
This is called courtship.

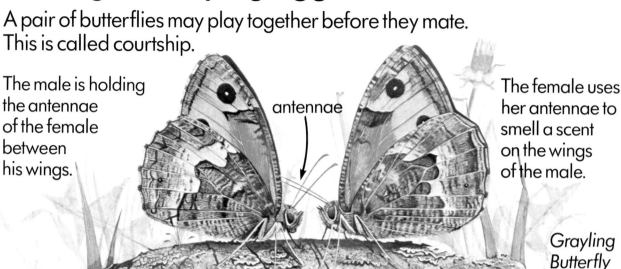

The male is holding the antennae of the female between his wings.

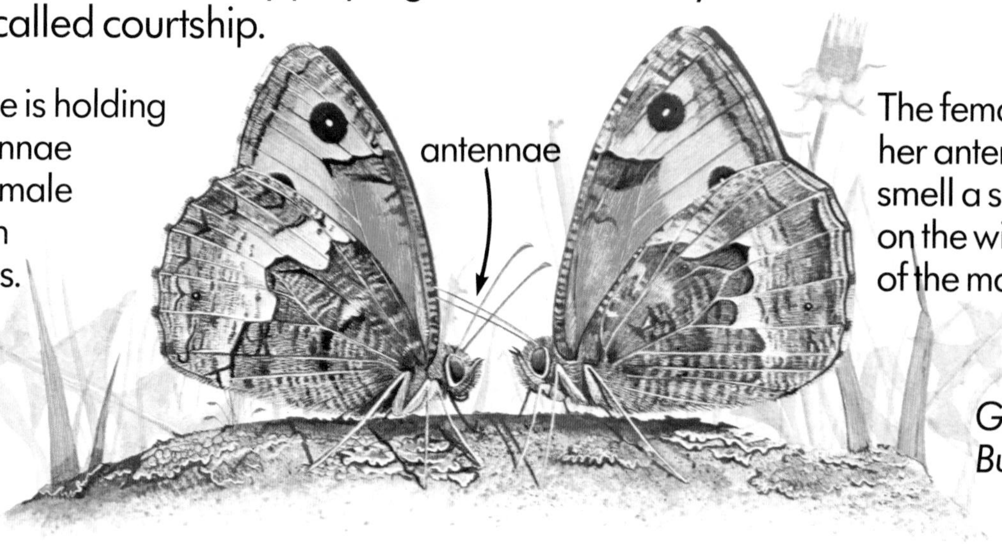

The female uses her antenna to smell a scent on the wings of the male.

Grayling Butterfly

When butterflies or moths mate, they join their abdomens together.
A bag of sperm passes from the male to the female.
The sperm joins with eggs inside the female.

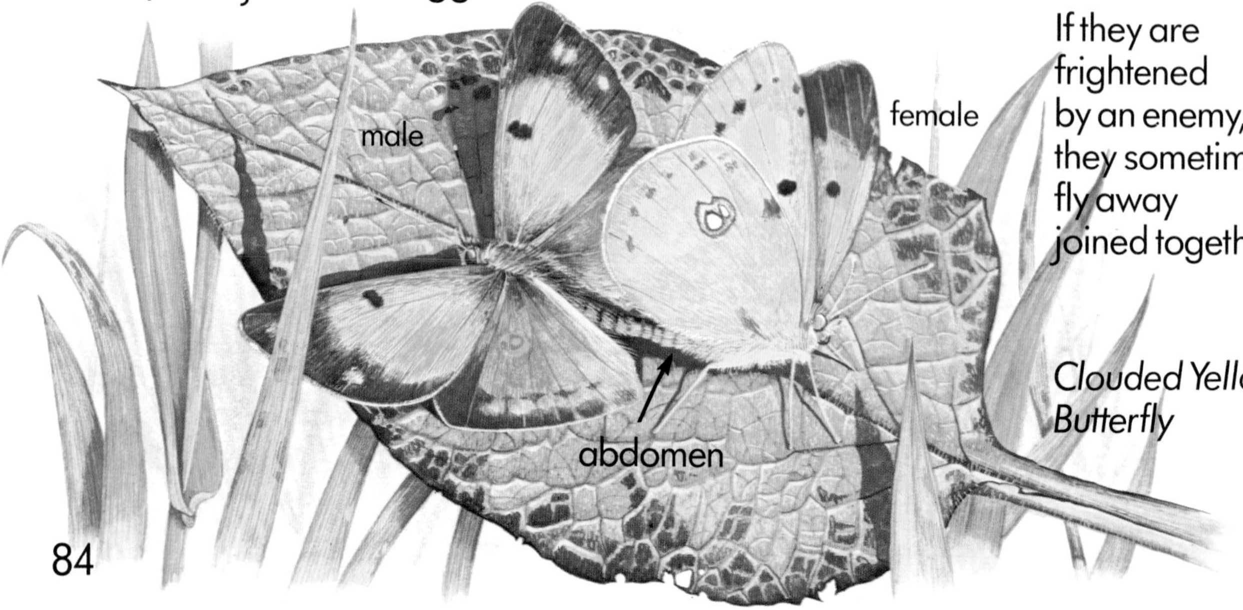

If they are frightened by an enemy, they sometimes fly away joined together.

Clouded Yellow Butterfly

A female may have hundreds of eggs inside her. She will lay her eggs when she has mated.

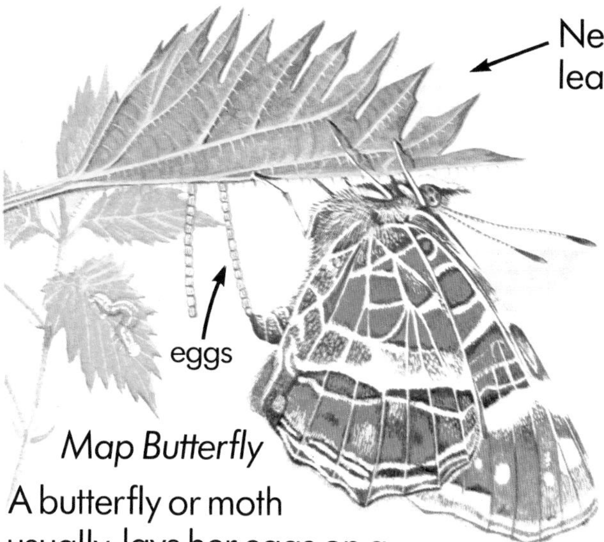

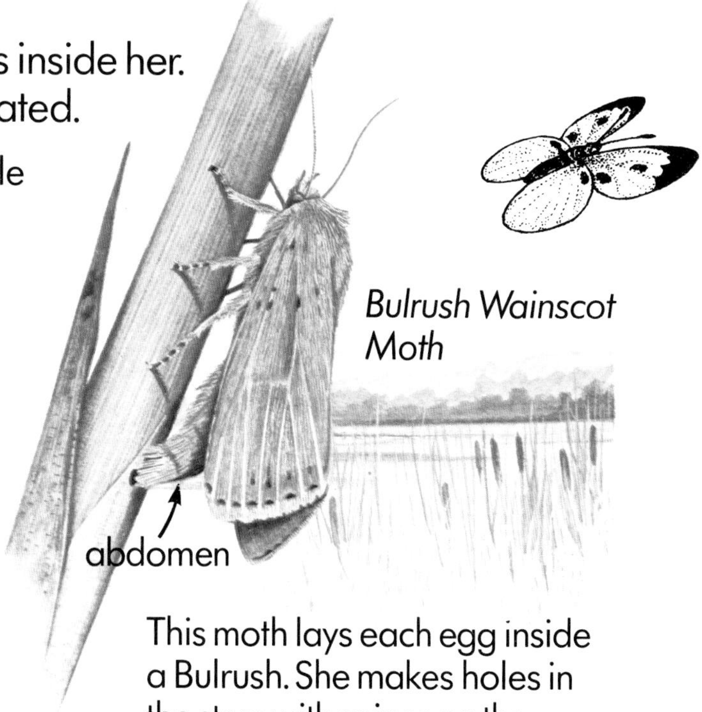

A butterfly or moth usually lays her eggs on a special plant. She can lay lots of eggs together, or one egg at a time.

This moth lays each egg inside a Bulrush. She makes holes in the stem with spines on the end of her abdomen.

This Moth sticks her eggs round a twig.

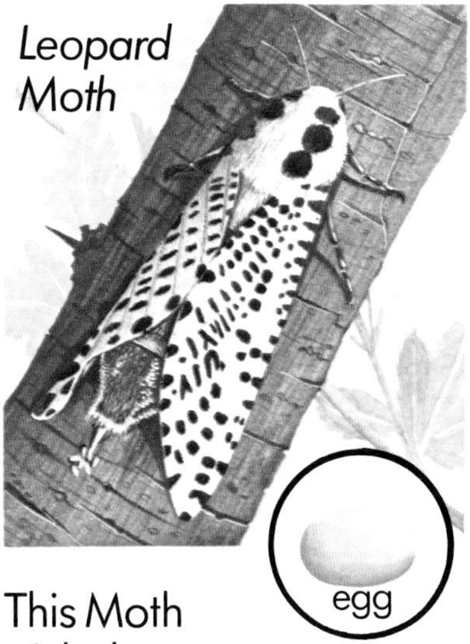

This Moth sticks her eggs on to tree bark.

This Butterfly lays her eggs as she flies.

The hungry caterpillar

Out of each egg comes a caterpillar. It eats and eats, and grows and grows. When it is big enough to start changing into an adult butterfly or moth, it stops growing.

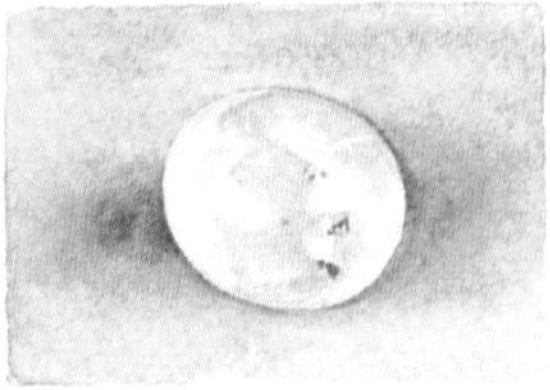

1. A moth caterpillar is inside this egg.

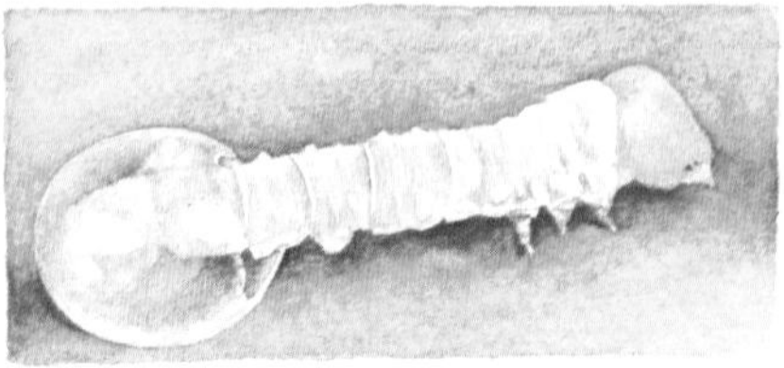

2. The caterpillar eats a hole in the egg and crawls out.

3. It is very hungry, so it eats the old egg shell.

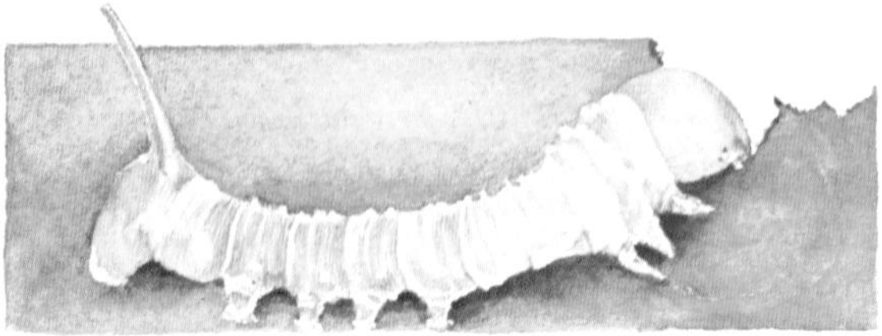

4. It eats the top of the leaf. Soon the caterpillar grows too big for its skin.

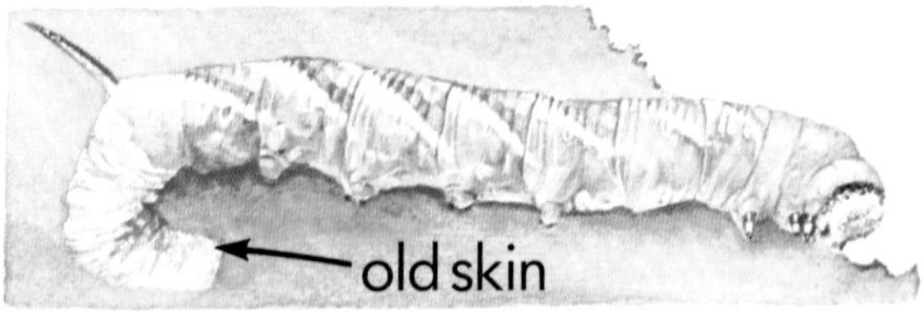

5. The skin splits and the caterpillar wriggles out. It is wearing a new skin.

6. The caterpillar eats Privet leaves. It eats and grows and eats and grows. It changes its skin three more times.

The caterpillar cannot see very well. It has twelve tiny eyes on its head. The eyes are too small for you to see.

Mouth parts for chewing.
The three pairs of front legs hold on to the food.
The five pairs of fleshy legs are called claspers. They can grip tightly to a stalk.
The caterpillar breathes through air holes in the side of its body. There is an air hole in the centre of each coloured spot.

Caterpillars and pupae

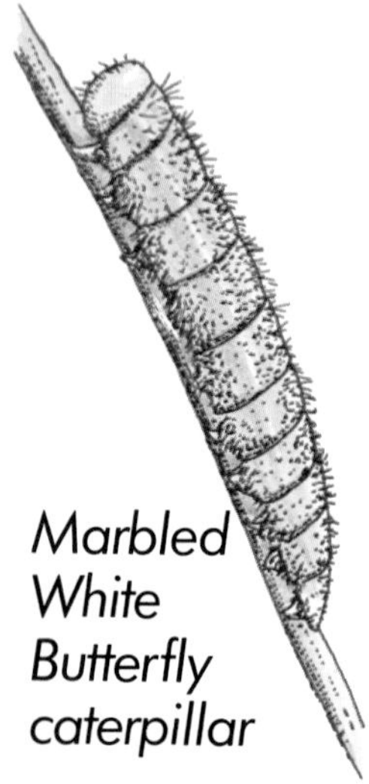

Marbled White Butterfly caterpillar

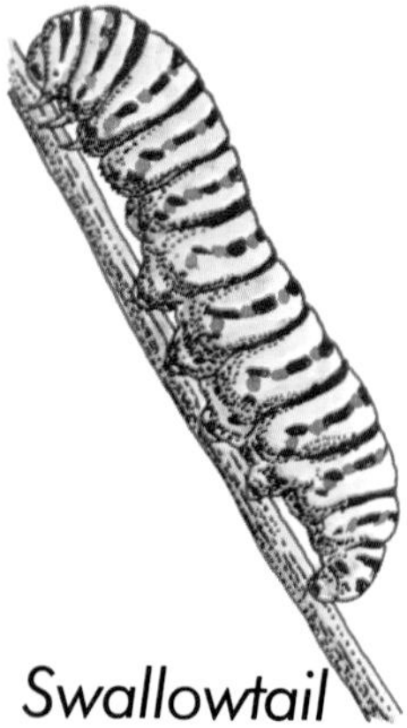

Swallowtail Butterfly caterpillar

This caterpillar makes a loop shape as it walks.

When some caterpillars rest, they look like twigs. This helps them to hide from their enemies.

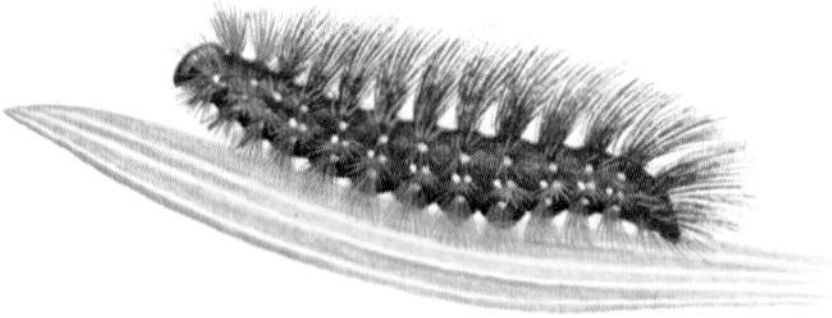

Some caterpillars are hairy. Birds do not like to eat them.

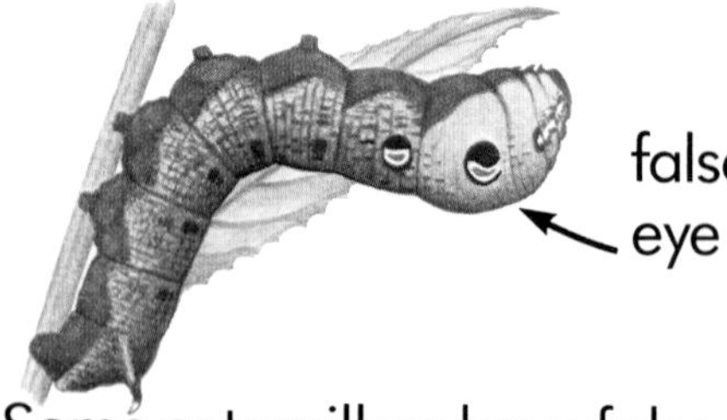

Some caterpillars have false eyes to frighten enemies.

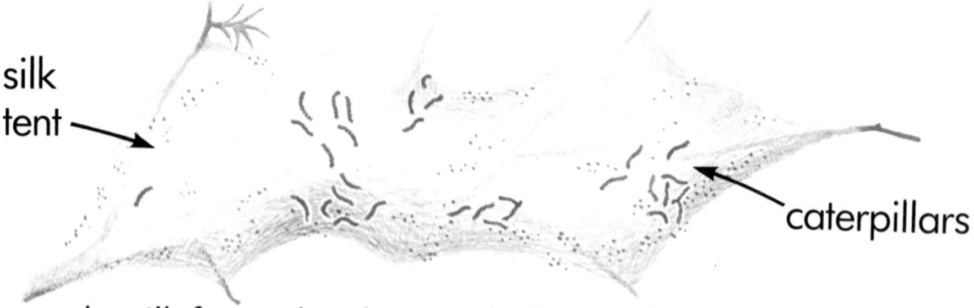

Caterpillars make silk from glands near their mouths. Some caterpillars use this silk to make tents to hide in.

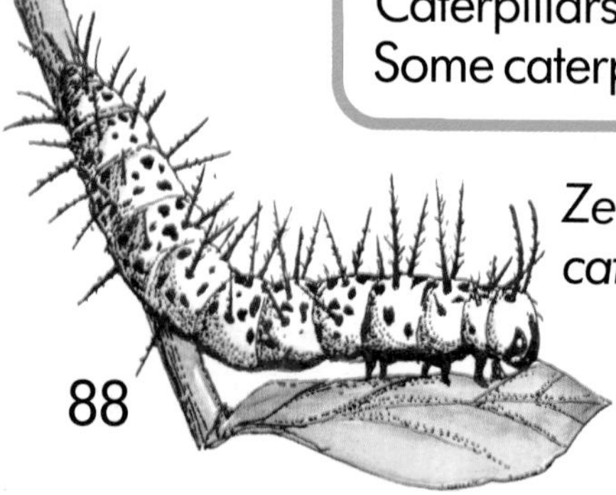

Zebra Butterfly caterpillar

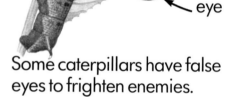

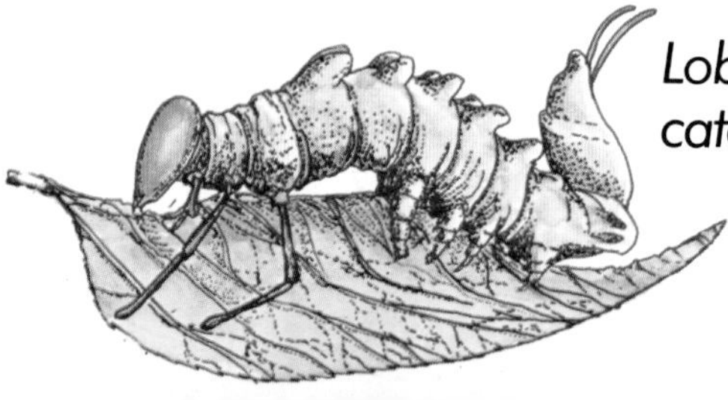

Lobster Moth caterpillar

When caterpillars are fully grown, they change into pupae.

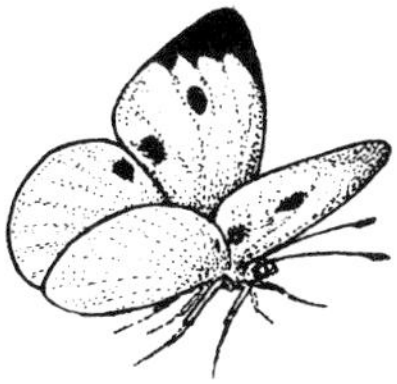

Peacock Butterfly caterpillar

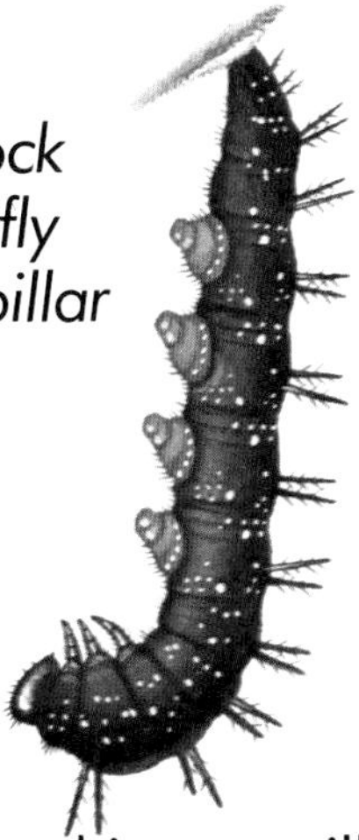

1. When this caterpillar is fully grown, it hangs upside down.

2. The caterpillar changes into a pupa inside its skin.

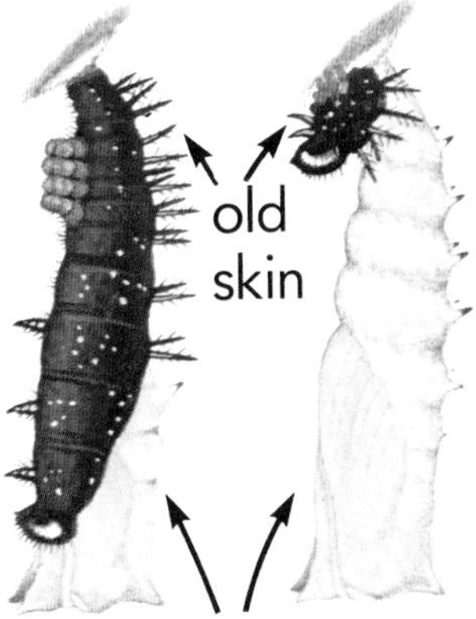

3. When the pupa wriggles, the skin splits. and slides up the pupa.

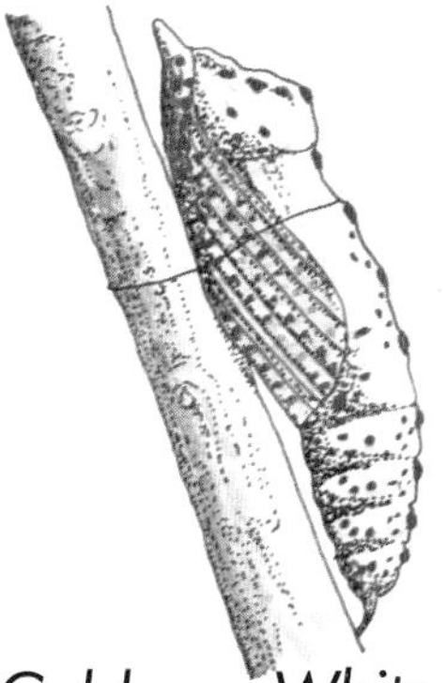

Cabbage White Butterfly pupa

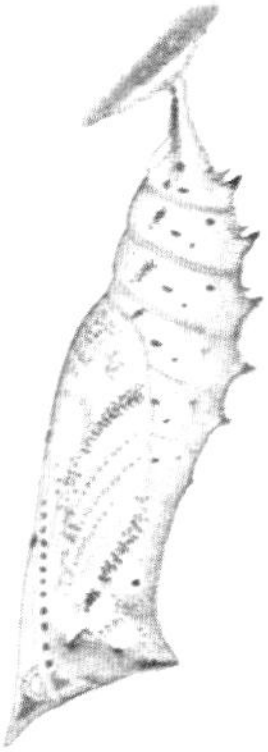

4. The pupa skin is now hard. It has changed colour.

Some moth caterpillars bury themselves in the ground. Then they change into pupae.

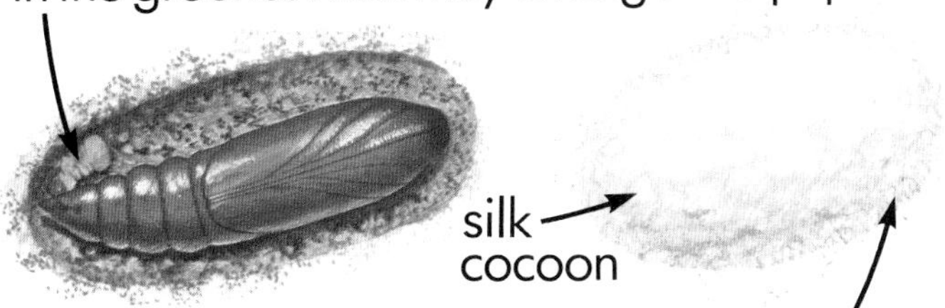

Some moth caterpillars spin silk cocoons around themselves. The caterpillars change into pupae inside the cocoons.

Bagworm Moth cocoon

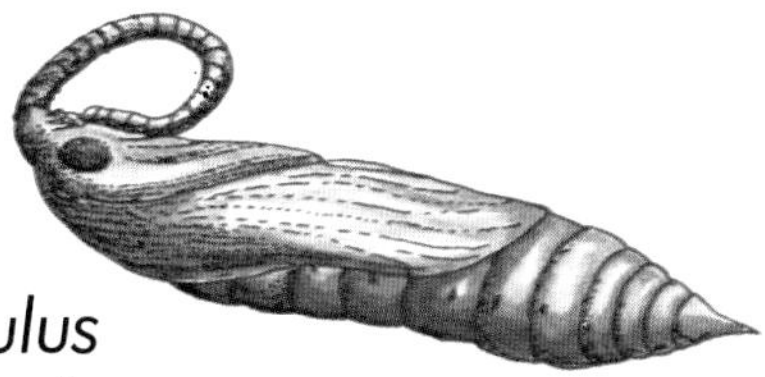

Convolvulus Hawk Moth pupa

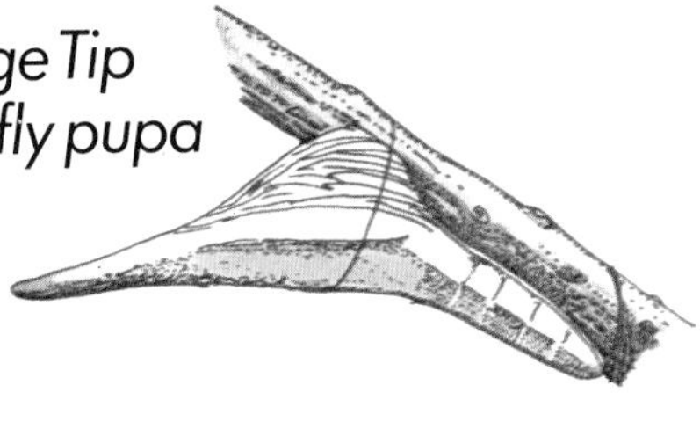

Orange Tip Butterfly pupa

The magic change

Inside a pupa, a butterfly or moth is being made.

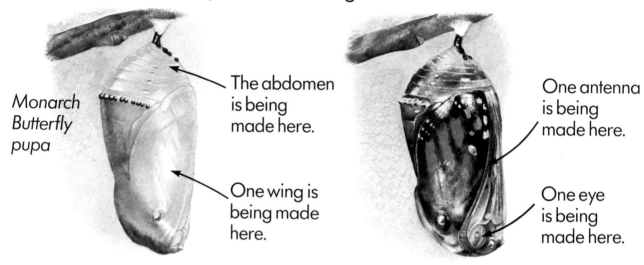

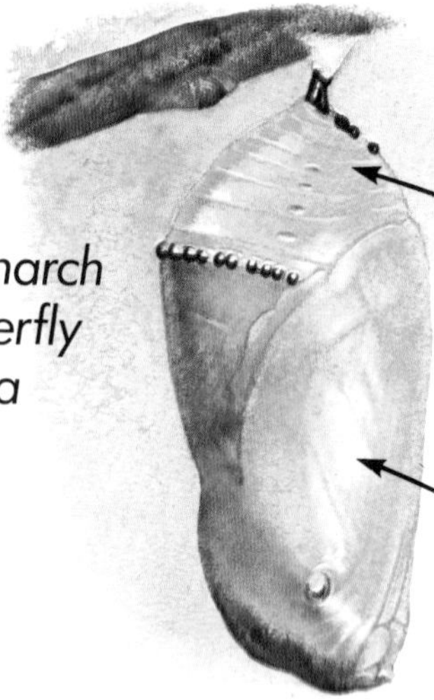

1. This pupa is two days old. A Monarch Butterfly is being made inside it.

One antenna is being made here.
One eye is being made here.

2. The pupa is now two weeks old. The Butterfly is nearly ready to come out.

The Butterfly is pulling out its antennae, legs and proboscis.

3. The pupa skin splits. The head and legs of the Butterfly come out first.

4. The Butterfly pulls out its abdomen. It pumps blood into the veins of its wings.

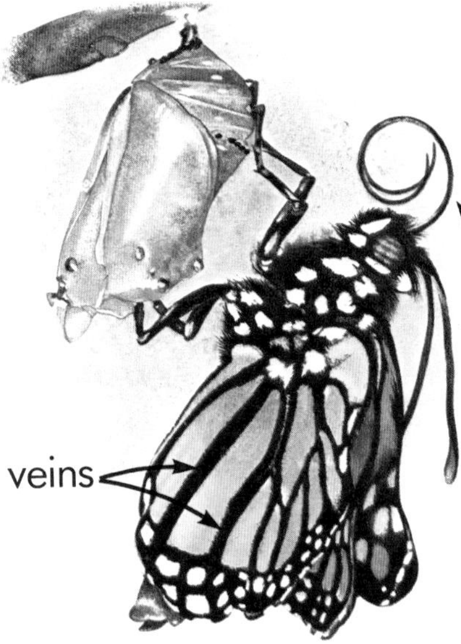

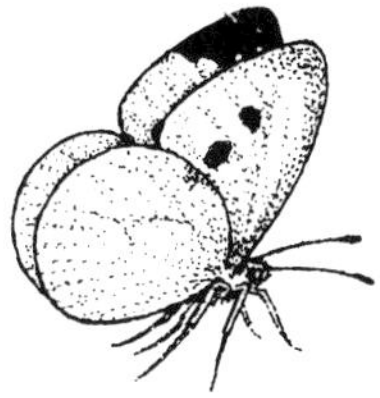

5. Blood is pumping from the abdomen into the veins. This makes the wings unfold.

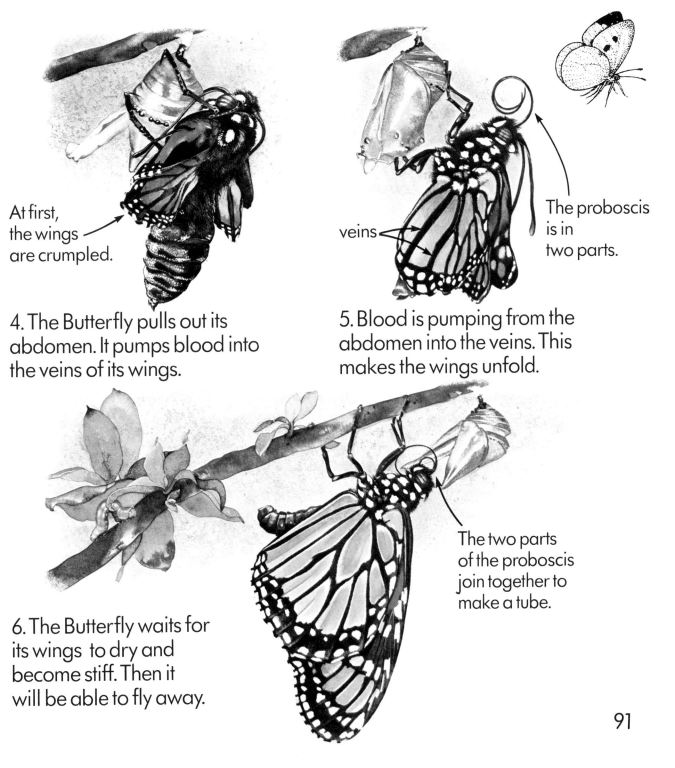

The two parts
of the proboscis
join together to
make a tube.

6. The Butterfly waits for its wings to dry and become stiff. Then it will be able to fly away.

How long do they live?

A butterfly or moth goes through four stages in its life. Adult butterflies and moths usually live only a few days or weeks. When they have mated and the female has laid her eggs, the adults die.

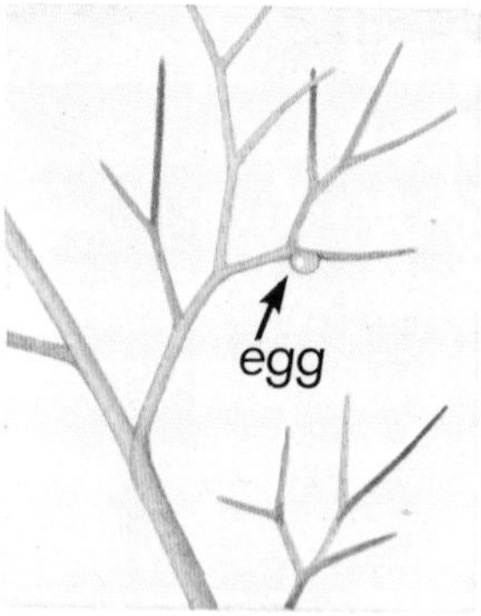

1. A butterfly or moth starts its life as an egg.

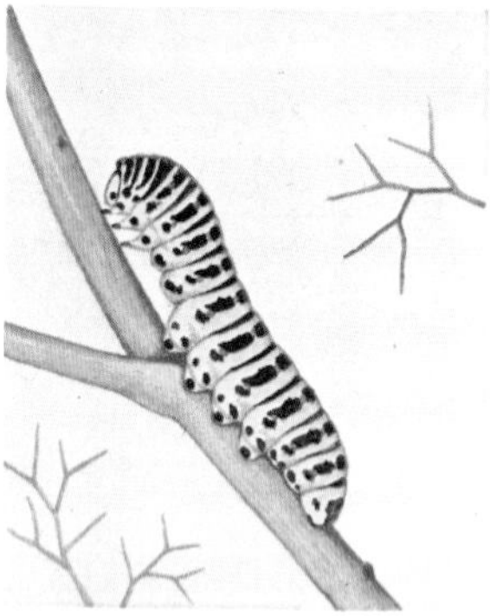

2. The egg changes into a caterpillar.

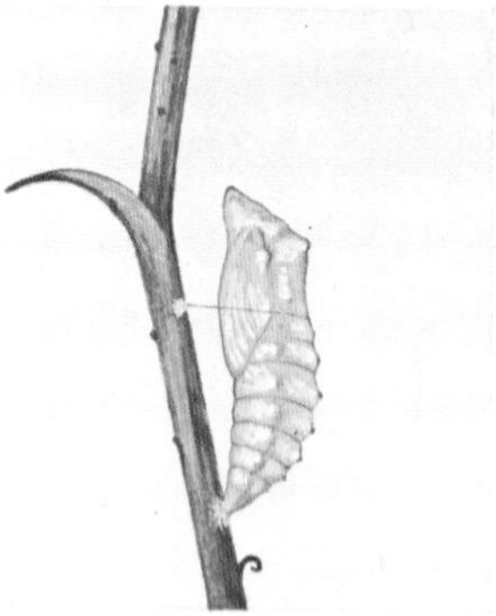

3. The caterpillar changes into a pupa.

4. The pupa changes into an adult.

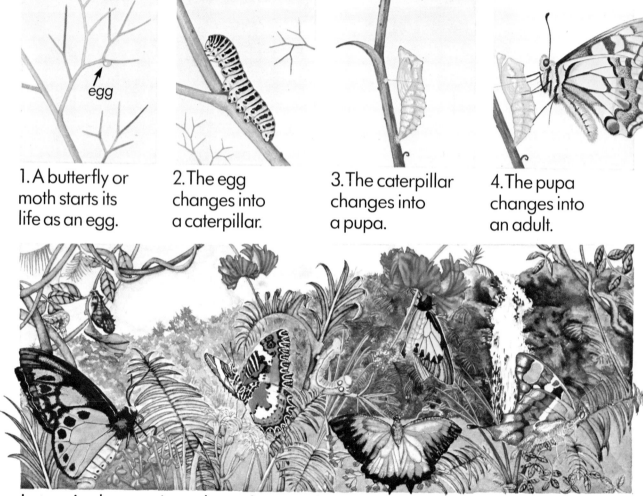

In tropical countries, where the weather is always hot, a butterfly or moth often takes only a few weeks to change from an egg into an adult.

In colder countries, a butterfly or moth may take several months to change from an egg to an adult. In countries with very cold winters, they go into a deep sleep. They wake up when the weather gets warmer.

The Lackey Moth spends the winter as an egg.
The Herald Moth sleeps through the winter as an adult.
The Cabbage White Butterfly spends the winter as a pupa.
The Privet Hawk Moth spends the winter as a pupa in the soil.
The Marbled White Butterfly sleeps through the winter as a young caterpillar.

Butterflies and moths that spend part of their lives sleeping through the winter may take a year to change from an egg to an adult.

Enemies

Butterflies and moths have lots of enemies.

Birds eat them.

Spiders eat them.

Insects eat them.

At night, many moths are eaten by bats.

Some moths have ears on the sides of their bodies. They help them to hear the squeaks that bats make. If these moths hear a bat coming, they drop to the ground or try to dodge out of the way.

Blue Underwing Moth

Some butterflies and moths have special colours. They use them to frighten away enemies.

Red Underwing Moth

If an enemy disturbs this moth, it opens and closes its wings. The flash of red may frighten away the enemy.

Owl Butterfly

This butterfly has false eyes on its wings. Birds may think they are the eyes of a dangerous animal.

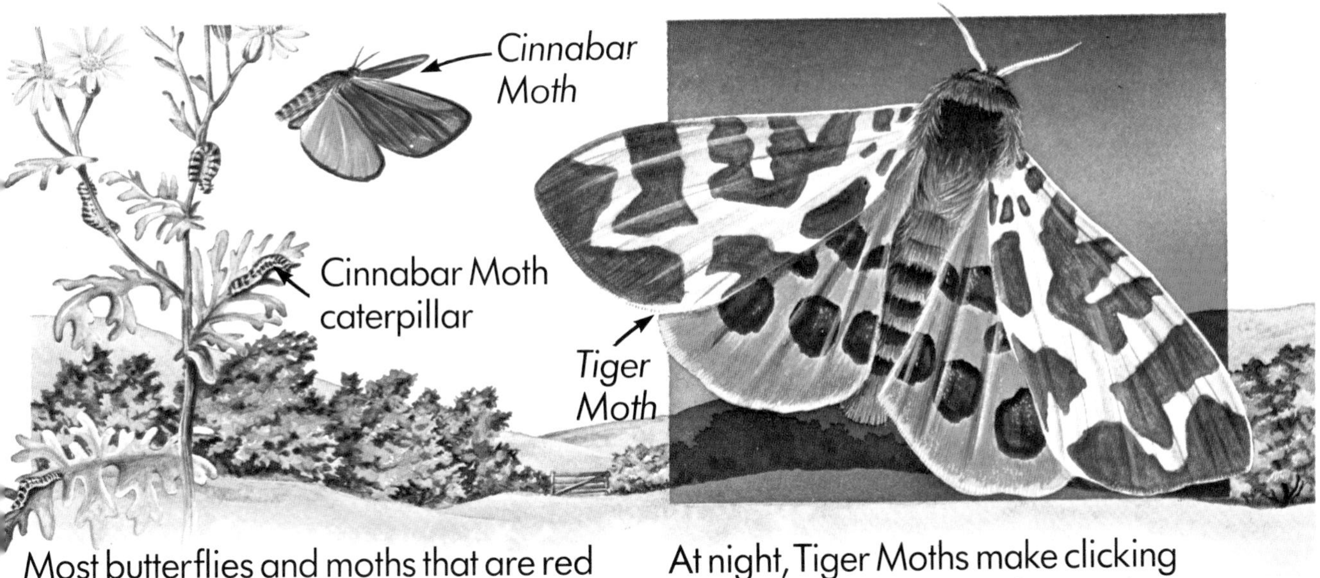

Most butterflies and moths that are red and black, or yellow and black, taste nasty. Birds learn to leave them alone.

At night, Tiger Moths make clicking noises. Bats soon learn that moths that make this noise taste bad.

INDEX

BIRDS

TREES

FLOWERS

FLOWERS
Continued

BUTTERFLIES